how to run a
great workshop

Books that make you better

Books that make you better. That make you *be* better, *do* better, *feel* better. Whether you want to upgrade your personal skills or change your job, whether you want to improve your managerial style, become a more powerful communicator, or be stimulated and inspired as you work.

Prentice Hall Business is leading the field with a new breed of skills, careers and development books. Books that are a cut above the mainstream – in topic, content and delivery – with an edge and verve that will make you better, with less effort.

Books that are as sharp and smart as you are.

Prentice Hall Business.
We work harder – so you don't have to.

For more details on products, and to contact us, visit
www.pearsoned.co.uk

Nikki Highmore Sims

how to run a
great workshop

The Complete Guide to
Designing and Running Brilliant
Workshops and Meetings

PEARSON
Prentice Hall
BUSINESS

Harlow, England • London • New York • Boston • San Francisco • Toronto
Sydney • Tokyo • Singapore • Hong Kong • Seoul • Taipei • New Delhi
Cape Town • Madrid • Mexico City • Amsterdam • Munich • Paris • Milan

PEARSON EDUCATION LIMITED

Edinburgh Gate
Harlow CM20 2JE
Tel: +44 (0)1279 623623
Fax: +44 (0)1279 431059
Website: www.pearsoned.co.uk

First published in Great Britain in 2006

© Nikki Highmore Sims 2006

The right of Nikki Highmore Sims to be identified as the author of this work has been asserted by her in accordance with the Copyright, Designs and Patents Act 1988.

ISBN: 978-0-273-70787-5

British Library Cataloguing-in-Publication Data
A catalogue record for this book is available from the British Library

Library of Congress Cataloging-in-Publication Data
Sims, Nikki Highmore.
   How to run a great workshop : the complete guide to designing and running brilliant workshops and meetings / Nikki Highmore Sims.
      p. cm.
   Includes index.
   ISBN-13: 978-0-273-70787-5 (alk. paper)
   ISBN-10: 0-273-70787-6 (alk. paper)
   1. Business presentations. 2. Workshops (Adult education) 3. Meetings. I. Title.
   HF5718.22.S564 2006
   651.7—dc22

                                                                    2006046802

12
14

Typeset in 11pt Minion by 70
Printed and bound in Malaysia (CTP-PPSB)

Contents

Chapter 4 Meetings makeover

Why choose this book?

If you're:

- a manager faced with running workshops, meetings, presentations or briefings; or

- a consultant, coach, therapist or self-employed businessperson who would like to add workshops to your repertoire; or

- someone who would like to design and run interactive group sessions

... then this book offers you a simple approach to creating and delivering a brilliant workshop (or any interactive group meeting).

WHAT THIS BOOK DOES

This process is specifically designed for people who use any kind of group session within their work, for example to:

- share skills, tools, information or processes with staff or key audiences;

- facilitate group tasks or processes;

- disseminate new information or policies;

- attract new clients or develop business with existing ones;

- hold regular updates on progress and projects.

If you read and *apply* (the essential part) the learning in this book, you will be able to:

- identify your 'natural' style of presentation, and adapt it to optimize your audience's learning capacity;

- present your workshop in the best possible way for optimum buy in;

- turn 'dry-as-dust' theory into interesting information that sticks;

- 'warm up' your audience even before they (or you) walk through the door and even if they've 'been sent';

- design activities that stimulate and appeal to your participants' different styles, rather than subjecting them to 'death by PowerPoint';

- pace your group session to ensure that the learning is highly interactive, in a way that doesn't ignore the fact that it also needs to be properly assimilated;

- ensure a demonstrable return on investment of time and cost;

- create and maintain a high level of energy and interest in the room – no post-lunch 'graveyard shifts'!

- turn evaluation into a painless, even enjoyable, informative process;

- transform the dullest training or meeting room into an oasis of learning;

- produce 'handouts' that are stimulating, effective and actually *used*;

- extend learning way beyond the duration of your session;

. . . and many, many more!

And not only can you use the processes, tools and tips to design highly interactive group sessions at work but you can also apply them to meetings, launches, networking, parties . . . even weddings (and I did)!

WHAT THIS BOOK DOESN'T DO

This book does not teach presentation skills or 'formal' training. The focus is, first, on really good design and, second, on delivery, with a highlight on tools you can use to embellish your own natural style of delivery. I don't include the following.

- How you stand/breathe/position your hands, etc. (I don't care if you sit, do headstands or jog on the spot – you'll still get the results you want if you follow the process).

- How to project your voice (you'll be getting the audience to do most of the talking) – though experiential training in this area is always useful.

- How to use 'proper' audio-visual equipment such as PowerPoint and overhead projectors – in fact I don't cover this at all other than a section on *why* I don't on pp. 148–9 (you'll be using 'live' media like flipcharts, walls, floors, people . . .).

- How to dress and project a suitable image (do it in fancy dress if you prefer – and for themed workshops that's even desirable).

- Learning theory that's primarily oriented towards trainers and teachers; this is a book for those using workshops as a tool rather than for a living, and there are many excellent books for trainers that cover this subject in depth.

My approach is informal and creative, but – fear not – soundly based on the latest in learning science and years of somewhat hazardous real-life experience (and experimentation).

In short, once you've got your head round the principles within this book, you will be able to deal with just about anything that is thrown at you in terms of designing and running effective group sessions.

Introduction

This book will help you create and conduct workshops, meetings and other group sessions that are so marvellously memorable, enjoyably effective and effortlessly engaging that your team will revere you, clients will adore you, your boss will promote you and your audience will want to have your babies (so to speak).

The process is in four sections.

- **Who, what, why and where** – you, what you want to achieve with your session and who your audience is – a good place to start for obvious reasons.

- **Whole-brain learning primer** – hands-on practical stuff that you'll be able to apply in your design and delivery, and other areas.

- **Building a great session** – a three-part section: first the framework and learning outcomes for each section; then detailed suggestions for exercises and tools to create a highly successful experience from start to finish; then finally the materials.

- **Meetings makeover** – a small but perfectly formed section with succinct tips on how to apply these principles to spread your success and effectiveness to meetings.

DESIGN V. DELIVERY

The greater emphasis of this book is on design for many reasons, including the following.

- There are certain principles behind good design that, once assimilated, should make any and all situations in which you are facilitating a group in any way (formally or informally, professionally or personally, parties or purpose) easier, more impactful, greater fun and more memorable; I even used them to design my own wedding day (and, yes, the guests *did* have activities to do!)

- Good design can cover a multitude of delivery weaknesses.

- Delivery skills are best learned experientially, whether through a course or direct experience. However, the tips and tools in this book will accelerate any level of expertise.

Depending on your level of experience and current need, the book is designed with a comprehensive contents list and index so that you can either work through it systematically or dip into relevant sections.

However you use it, the aim of the book is to guide you towards putting together workshops that are fun to design, easy to deliver, fulfil your expectations, get the required results and make you look like you've been doing it all your life!

CHAPTER ONE

Who, what, why and where

YOUR NATURAL STYLE

This bit is about you: what are you like? What's your style? What kind of session would *you* like to run? Are you happy at the front of the room talking to a group of people; or do you prefer to be more facilitative, set up exercises for them to do then mingle and coach them through it?

The most important thing about running any kind of session is that, first, *you* enjoy it. If you're genuinely enjoying the session and your subject, then a lot of the work is done in terms of engaging your audience.

Figure 1.1 illustrates three workshop facilitation styles, ranging from less to more interactive, with descriptions. Consider them all and tick any and all aspects that instinctively appeal to you. It will help you with the design and layout (not to mention delivery) of the workshop if you can incorporate elements that feel naturally right for you.

One point: you will notice a bias in this book towards a more facilitative, interactive style – this is simply because it's the one that helps people learn more, faster (not to mention stay awake longer), and also it's usually the easiest on even the most nervous of first-time facilitators once you know how to let the structure of the session do most of the work.

However, even if your natural style is 'lecturer', there are many tips on how to find the right balance for you and your group.

My own personal style is something like a blend of 5 per cent lecturer, 30 per cent trainer and 65 per cent facilitator. What's yours?

Figure 1.1 Delivery styles

Lecturer/info sharer	Trainer/leader	Facilitator/coach
Characteristics ❏ Stays mostly 'up front' (90–100%) ❏ Usually perceived as an 'expert' in some subject ❏ Majority of input is through verbal explanation and models on visual aids ❏ Could well be a very good public speaker and engaging ❏ Usually standing slight distance away at head of group and group sitting in rows, sometimes tables ❏ Little or no flexibility in session to respond to group need or change **Materials** ❏ Visual aids will be PowerPoint, overhead projectors (OHPs), video/film, flipcharts (more rarely) ❏ Handouts will often be text heavy ❏ No visuals on walls or elsewhere, or used by group during presentation **Model** ❏ Model of imparting knowledge ❏ Little or no hands-on application from audience ❏ Questions usually at end as a formal debrief	**Characteristics** ❏ Stays mostly up front (60–80%) but much more moving around/involvement with participants ❏ Doesn't have to be necessarily an 'expert', but will be expected to walk the talk ❏ Majority of input is verbal, with some demonstrations and discussion-based exercises or group debate ❏ More interactivity means less emphasis on skills as a public speaker and greater flexibility to respond to change or group need ❏ Usually at head of group standing or perched on work table, with group sitting in a horseshoe, 'cabaret style' or boardroom **Materials** ❏ More likely to see flipcharts being used interactively ❏ Other visual aids (PowerPoint, etc.) ❏ Might be some additional materials handed round or around room or used during exercises ❏ Participants might have handbooks to work from during workshop or to take away **Model** ❏ Model of sharing knowledge ❏ Fairly hands-on, so suitable for knowledge and skills training ❏ Questions at end of sections or during	**Characteristics** ❏ Can be up front, middle, part of group, move around – no 'locus of authority' ❏ Only expertise necessary is facilitation skills ❏ Some verbal input (20–30%), but mostly in the form of outlining exercises, framing subjects, discussion and debriefs ❏ Highly hands-on and interactive; facilitator working a lot one-to-one or one-to-group during exercises ❏ Might sit in a circle with the group or horseshoe but on same level **Materials** ❏ Likely to be a wide range of visual, auditory and kinaesthetic materials involved in exercises ❏ Visual aids most likely to be flipcharts and posters, etc. ❏ Handbooks or handouts are likely to be interactive **Model** ❏ Model of sharing experience and skills ❏ Very hands-on, so suitable for skills training ❏ High level of input and participation required from group ❏ Questions encouraged throughout

Scores:
Lecturer   /12   Trainer   /12   Facilitator   /12

As you can see, there's quite a range of delivery styles and interactivity, and while people very generally tend to fall mainly into one of these three, the best blend is a tailored mix that suits your personality and the group you're working with.

Style development

Lecturer/information sharer

If you feel at this point that your natural style is, or has been, more lecturer than anything, ask yourself the following questions (and answer them honestly – I'm not looking!)

1 Do you believe that formal delivery is the best way to impart important facts and knowledge? (If so, please see pp. 36–47 – 'All you need to know about learning theory'.)

2 Do you feel most comfortable with this style because it involves just being in control of your own notes/presentation and speaking about what you know best, without having to get involved with things like group dynamics and managing exercises – out of which you have no idea what will come? (If so, please see pp. 35–6 – 'The biggest myth in training'.)

3 Is it because the information that has to be imparted is highly specific and the only way to get it across accurately is through step-by-step explanation and clear notes? (If so, please see pp. 30–4 – 'Information v. learning')

Yes, I'm fairly unsubtly and wholly unashamedly trying to encourage you to adopt a more interactive approach to workshops. Why? Because the brain learns better that way, so your information will be more effectively taken up and used; participants enjoy them more, so they're more likely to ask you back; and it's actually more enjoyable to deliver.

Trainer/leader

If you feel your natural style is more trainer/leader than anything else, ask yourself the following questions (and, again, answer them honestly!)

1 Do you love the idea of being 'up front' and the life and soul of the room, with confidence that you can get across all you need to? (If so, please see pp. 36–47 – 'All you need to know about learning theory'.)

2 Do you think that the best way to get people to learn is to explain something, then get them to discuss it, and have a mop-up debrief afterwards? (If so, please see Chapter 2 – 'Whole-brain learning primer' – for a host of other ways that involve more of the brain.)

3 Are your standard materials A4 handouts at the end of the workshop or each session that summarize key points? (If so, see pp. 161–4 – 'Materials' – for ideas that could save you time and money as well as get even better results.)

Here, I'm addressing the more dyed-in-the-wool Training style (the capital T denotes a more formal style often unflatteringly labelled 'chalk and talk'), which uses the more traditional methods of training. Though it's more interactive than lecturing, it still errs towards passive rather than active learning. Once again I'm encouraging movement towards an even more interactive approach, for the same reasons as given for the lecturer style, though this style still has a place as it is one of the ways to give participants a 'breather' from activity and therefore time to assimilate information.

Facilitator/coach

Once again, try these questions if you feel your natural style is more facilitator/coach and be honest.

1 Do you shudder at the thought of having to 'present' anything, far preferring to be part of the group and share experiences? (If so, see pp. 5–10 – 'Beliefs and the importance of make-believe' – for alternative ways you could think about facilitation that would allow you to lead the group more often.)

2 Do you believe that everyone has something to teach, and you learn as much from your group as they do from you? (If so, see pp. 19–20 – 'What type of session?' – since this is closer to a co-coaching or support group than a workshop.)

3 Do you believe that all learning should be entirely experiential and hands-on? (If so, see pp. 45–7 – 'Honey and Mumford's four learning styles'.)

This time, just to be awkward, I'm advocating adding in a little more of a trainer approach. In my experience, it's possible to be *too* interactive; some people do need some reflective time and passive input, and a non-stop romp of activity can leave them behind, bewildered and be-reath-less. It's also about defining your market and your offering; not all workshops are created equal – as the section on p. 19 ('What type of session?') sets out, some are really support or coaching groups.

BELIEFS AND THE IMPORTANCE OF MAKE-BELIEVE

Before we take another step, let's consider what you currently believe about your audience, yourself as the person about to deliver the group session . . . and also the session itself.

What have beliefs[1] got to do with running a workshop? Heaps.

We cannot always (even often) control what happens around us, but we *can* massively influence how we *respond* to what happens (inside and out), and therefore what *then* happens as a result of our response. In this way, we all have far more control in general than we think.

In terms of running workshops, this means we have a large amount of influence on how we'll feel leading up to it, while conducting it and towards our participants (even the 'difficult' ones). In fact, managing our beliefs can even result in fewer, if any, 'difficult' participants.

Very simplistically, what happens between an event and our reaction to it is this:

We receive a stimulus (event, look, comment) → it passes through the 'filter' of our beliefs about that person/situation → we interpret the stimulus accordingly → we respond internally (thought or reaction) or externally (comment or action).

---

[1] The word 'beliefs' in this context means the way in which you're thinking about anything, irrespective of whether it's 'true' or not. So it can include preconceptions, assumptions, hearsay, 'truth', 'reality' or even make-believe.

To illustrate, imagine the following.

[**Stimulus**] You catch your boss looking at you thoughtfully →

[**Belief**] Someone just told you that your boss hated your last presentation →

[**Meaning**] You interpret the look to mean your boss is wondering how to tell you the bad news →

[**Response**] Your heart sinks and you start wondering whether this could jeopardize your place on the new project . . .

To take this to the next stage, your response then becomes your boss's stimulus:

You're looking completely fed up →

Your boss had *actually* been thinking of coming over to praise your latest presentation, it was so impressive →

Your boss interprets your expression to mean you're stressed at the moment →

So your boss decides to let you work and find a better time instead

And now . . .

Your boss looks down at the work on the desk →

You think your boss can't even look at you, the presentation was that bad →

Despair turns to anger and you become incensed that your boss can't even tell you to your face →

So you leap to your feet to go and have it out with your boss . . .

Ad infinitum.

When you understand the role that our beliefs, assumptions, expectations (call them what you will) play in our responses and behaviour, it's fairly easy to see why so many communications break down. People aren't at all responding to what actually happens, but to their *interpretation* of what happened – and that is determined by their *beliefs* about the situation or person at that moment. This is the root of the so-called 'self-fulfilling prophecy'.

If colleagues or clients ever offer (or start) to tell you about a 'trouble-maker' in a group you're going to facilitate, stop them. It could unconsciously colour your perceptions of that person, allowing him or her to fulfil the role of troublemaker nicely. On the other hand, if you instead choose to assume that everyone in the group (a) wants to be there (whether or not this is the 'truth') and (b) is contributing positively with everything he or she does/says, this can be a highly effective way of carrying that 'troublemaker' along with the group and in some cases turning him or her round completely. He or she will have been so used to being treated like a 'difficult person' that an entirely different approach can lead to an entirely different behaviour.

Useful beliefs

The key factor in whether a belief is useful or not is: how does it make you feel? If you feel good when you think it, it's a useful belief. If not, it might be worth trying another one.

If you're not even sure right now what you believe, you can still go well prepared – no matter what the group or subject.

Here are some basic useful beliefs I find particularly helpful, no matter what the group, subject, how I feel or what day it is I'm working.

- I love working with groups.
- This group is going to *love* this ('this' being whatever you're offering).
- I can't wait to meet everyone.
- This is going to be really enjoyable.
- I'm going to make a real positive difference today.
- What we're doing is really useful and I believe in it.
- I love this stuff (this is a very useful, deliberately vague, mantra that, when repeated to yourself regularly before, during and after any session, seems to add a glow of positivity to any situation).

In a moment there's a chance for you to create a bunch of your own. None of them have to be 'true', by the way – and, in fact, some can even be demonstrably 'false'.

Example

Once I had to give a presentation to a group of people who had been presented to twice before on the same subject (it was a training proposal), and both times they'd thrown it out. They also weren't 'trainer-friendly', and I knew this. Added to which, while waiting in the corridor to be called into the room, I was passed by a colleague who came back, asked me what I was waiting to do and, on hearing what it was, burst into disbelieving laughter and snorted 'Good luck!' with all the sincerity of someone saying 'Have fun' to a friend about to enter the dentist's.

So what did I do? Flying in the face of logic and possibly even sanity, I went in radiating the 'knowledge' that they were going to love it and, lo and behold, they accepted the proposal without a quibble. My colleagues accused me of drugging the group.

Being conscious of how you are thinking about your group, workshop and – most importantly – yourself in the role of session facilitator or leader is one of the most essential skills you can develop.

The following exercise gives you a basic starting point for this, but it might really pay dividends if you were to extend this kind of thinking to other areas of your life.

Because it's often the case that we can think more easily what we don't want before what we do, we'll do this in a three-step way.

1 First, think about what you currently believe about your group/self/subject that you'd like to change.

2 Then, simply invent a better belief and try it on.

3 Finally, run the new belief through the Positive Beliefometer (tm!) to see how many boxes it ticks.

Exercise

Changing beliefs

Current belief/expectation	More useful belief

Positive Beliefometer*

When trying out your new belief, ideally it should make you:

❏ feel excited about the event, interaction or task;

❏ easily able to imagine yourself enjoying it;

❏ look forward to undertaking it;

❏ feel confident about the result and your abilities;

❏ more focused on the result and outcomes and less on the steps leading up to it.

If it doesn't tick all of those boxes, fine-tune it until it does.

Note: * According to the Gospel of Nikki, feel free to write your own internal checklist, but keep it centred on how you feel (yes, even you highly cerebral logical types!) when you think of the situation for which you want to find the belief.

By now you should have a set of beliefs that, when you think of them and imagine them to be true (and, by the way, the more you do this, the more likely it is they will become true), make you look forward to getting stuck into the workshop, meeting that group and generally having a great time.

Success ritual

Many 'performers' (and running a workshop definitely qualifies), whether in sport, the media or in business, have a 'success ritual' they use before each performance. I don't mean anything as elaborate as candles and chanting (though feel free, if that appeals), but a structured behaviour that helps them get into a peak state of mind and which can be a very powerful way of reinforcing your chosen beliefs.

Here's what I do, after the room's fully set up so all distractions are out of the way.

- Take a couple of deep breaths and 'centre' myself – by which I mean do whatever feels right to feel calm, relaxed (shoulders fully dropped) and present (bringing racing thoughts back to the moment).

- Picture the end of the workshop clearly: see people smiling, hear them thank me for an interesting and useful day, feel pleased with the way it's gone. Take a few moments to enjoy the feeling of success and my positive beliefs about the session 'coming true'.

- Feel gratitude for the way the workshop has 'been' such a success.

That's it! It takes around five minutes maximum and I find it a great way of relaxing and looking forward to the day ahead.

SESSION SUBJECT AND OUTCOMES

Subject

First, what's your subject? Is it one that's been handed to you or one of your choosing?

The first thing I do with any workshop is plonk my subject heading down on the middle of a page and 'mindmap'[2] quickly what I already know about it. That effectively becomes a brain dump that I add to as ideas occur and can be a useful starting and building point for the design.

Figure 1.2 presents an example of one of my mindmaps to give you an idea of how basic it can be and still work.

Outcomes

Even when (especially when?) the session subject and its main outcomes have been foisted upon you, it's still worth deciding for yourself what you would like to get out of it – for both yourself and your participants.

Generally it can be useful to separate these outcomes into public and personal. Why this is useful is because the outcomes will often determine – or suggest – the number and duration of the session(s), as well as the format. You may even find you don't need to run a workshop to achieve some of them – for example, coaching or a project supported by co-, group coaching or action learning sets might cover them (see pp. 19–20 for the different types of group sessions).

Public outcomes

1 What's the purpose of your group session or workshop?
   Try to encapsulate it in one sentence, stating the overall benefit(s) of attending. For example: 'I want to run a workshop that will demystify project management'.

2 What key skills, tools or knowledge do you want your participants to take away from it?
   As well as the 'official' ones you have to cover, include any you'd like them to take away. Think in terms of what they'll have learned, solved and/or gained. For example: 'They will have: (i) a relevant and valuable tool that they can take straight back to work and use; (ii) a clear supported plan for using it; (iii) solved an issue slowing their team's success'.

---

[2] For an excellent introduction to the subject of mindmapping, see Tony Buzan's book listed in the Resources section at the end of this book.

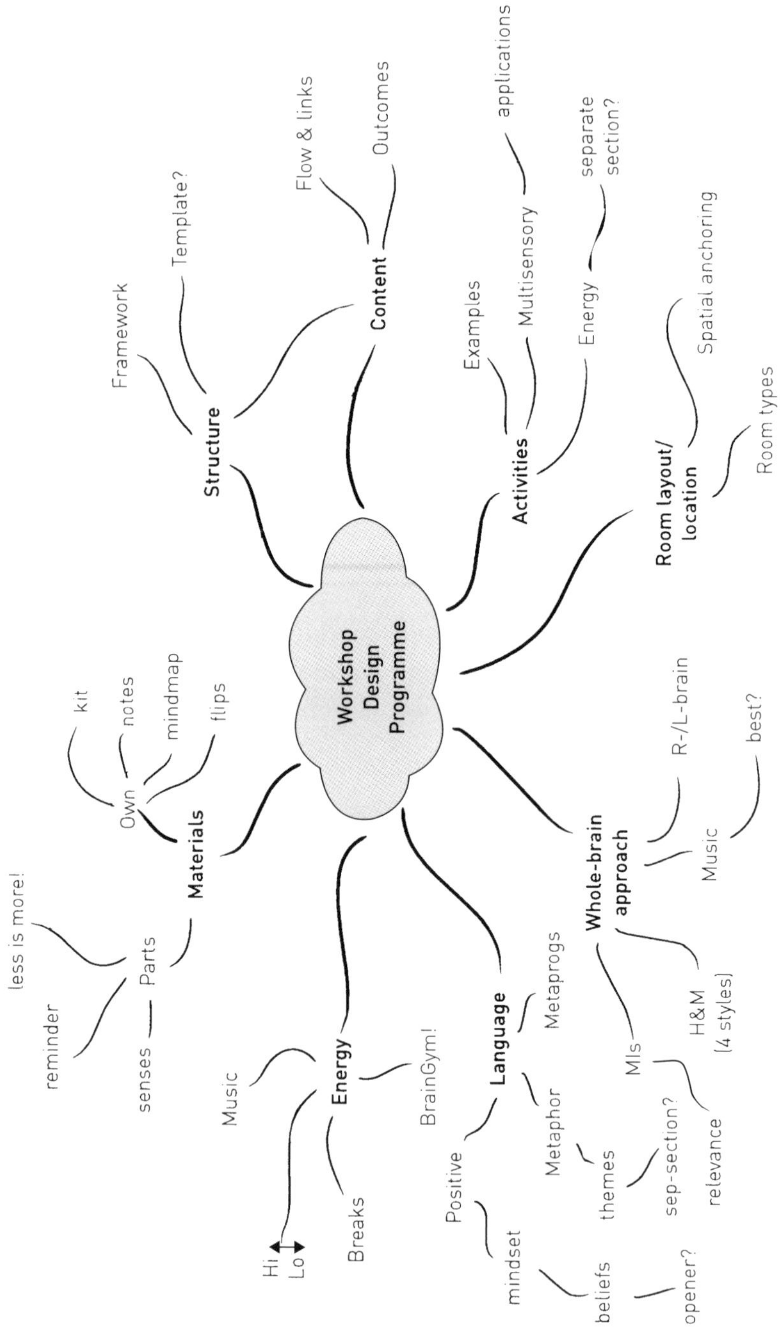

Figure 1.2 Example mindmap

A mindmap centred on "Workshop Design Programme" with the following branches and sub-branches:

- **Structure**
  - Framework
    - Template?
  - Flow & links
- **Content**
  - Outcomes
- **Activities**
  - Examples
  - Multisensory
    - applications
  - Energy
    - separate section?
- **Room layout/location**
  - Spatial anchoring
  - Room types
- **Whole-brain approach**
  - R-/L-brain
  - Music
    - best?
  - H&M (4 styles)
  - MIs
- **Language**
  - Metaprogs
  - Metaphor
    - themes
  - sep-section?
    - relevance
  - opener?
  - mindset
  - beliefs
- **Energy**
  - BrainGym!
  - Positive
  - Hi / Lo
  - Breaks
  - Music
- **Materials**
  - Parts
    - senses
    - reminder
    - less is more!
  - Own
    - kit
    - notes
    - mindmap
    - flips

3 Now go back to those outcomes and add in when, where and with whom.

For example: 'By the end of this session/within one month . . . in the office/with clients . . . when on the telephone, during sales meetings',
etc.

What *else* do you want it to do? Personal outcomes

Now for the personal outcomes: what you want to get for *yourself*. For example, 'I want to have fun, feel comfortable, make them laugh, get them to recommend me to their colleagues', etc.

So . . . what are your *personal* outcomes for your session, now that you think about it? What would you *like* it to bring you, even if not directly related to its topic? Again, this is equally (arguably more) useful to do if the subject/workshop has been dropped on you to ensure you also get something out of it.

1 What do you want?

Encapsulate your own outcome in one sentence if possible. For
example: 'I want to run the most successful and effective project
management workshop ever seen in my organization'.

2 How will you know you've achieved it?

When answering this, think about what you will see, hear and be
feeling or doing. For example: 'I will hear people saying they feel
inspired, see them getting really stuck into their mini-projects, and I
will be wandering around coaching individuals and small groups as
they work'.

3 What effects will it have on you, your team, your colleagues, your family, etc.?

Consider the ramifications (positive and negative, if applicable) of the
workshop, and particularly of making a huge success of it. For
example, 'As a result of this I'll be asked to lead other workshops across
the organization, giving me the chance to develop Sarah as my deputy
in my absence' . . . or 'I'll be asked to run workshops all over the
country, meaning I'll be away from home a lot more'.

If some negative thoughts come up in point 3, all you need to do is revisit your original outcome(s) and tweak it where necessary.

Now you have both your public and personal outcomes, you can start to see what is achievable in a group session and what is not. They will also help you design a session that you will enjoy as much as your participants – an important point. Sometimes they can also be separated out from the main workshop into pre- and post-session work or materials, lessening the 'delivery load'.

WHY BOTHER? APPLICATION OF LEARNING

How many times have you attended interesting meetings, briefings and workshops yet once you're back in the 'real world' just don't get sufficient time to make sure you put the new skills into practice?

Along with considering what you want to achieve with your workshop or group session, if you and your participants are truly to get the most out of your time spent together it's both best practice and commercial sense to consider exactly *how* they will be applying the learning or new information gained. Whether it's your own team, another organization or the general public, unapplied learning is a waste of time and money.

Benefits include:

- maintained momentum;

- reinforced learning;

- motivation to apply the learning/knowledge;

- increased organization's or client's return on investment;

- prolonged contact time with your group, giving you a better chance to build relationships and help them;

- vastly improved effectiveness of your session;

- showing you care about their outcomes;

- helping them take responsibility for what happens next.

Some questions to prompt your thinking about how you might encourage application.

1 If it's a process or tool, how will it be applied back in the workplace straight away?

2 If skills, when and how will they be used? What other dependent factors are involved, such as time to apply/use them, line management, colleagues' cooperation?

3 If knowledge, how will you know they've understood all your points, and how will they remember them beyond the session?

4 If the session is to create change of some kind, when do you expect your participants to make those changes, and what support will they need or can you offer?

Using 'projects' to apply the learning

Setting up real-life projects is a really effective way of helping your participants apply their learning/knowledge easily. They can be either in cross-functional teams (great way of promoting intra-organizational working and communication) or individual.

If you're working as a consultant, coach or other independent adviser, this is a good subject to agree with your clients as it gives them a chance to be actively involved in the design, helps them set the direction for how they want to measure the return on investment, and brings the intervention much closer to business issues than a lot of 'soft skills' training (if indeed you're working with 'soft skills').

By 'project', it doesn't have to be a huge thing – it can be as small as applying a new set of communication skills to the next ten people you talk to on the phone, then summarizing the results for a feedback session two or three weeks later.

The smallest 'project' could be another person's 'action plan' . . . but the difference, and what makes it a 'project', is that there will be some check-in point. This could be a teleconference to share results, a half-day workshop to develop skills further, a team meeting – the format isn't important, it's the deadline and sharing with others that makes it effective.

Setting up project groups, along with follow-up of some kind, allows your participants to implement those good intentions with the added support and incentive of having others around with a similar focus.

Setting up a 'project'

Some guidelines to consider when setting up a project and project groups – whether working with participants directly or with your organization or client.

1 Work closely with the key stakeholder and/or participants beforehand to establish what is realistic in terms of their own workload – there's no point in setting up a huge expectation that will stress them out! The key purpose of the project is *painless* application of learning, not unnecessary workload.

2 Set a realistic time frame of three to six weeks for accomplishment of the main goal or first milestone if it's a long-term project.

3 Suggest they choose an area that's close to them and which personally affects them or, if the area is determined by your organization or client, then build in an exercise during your session that helps to make those links.

4 Encourage cross-functional project groups wherever possible: it reduces 'silo' working, improves interdepartmental communication, enhances working relationships and increases creative output.

5 If possible, speak to a key stakeholder beforehand to establish what areas would make the most difference to the organization and include them as project success criteria. If working with individuals (e.g. the public), this comes under point 2.

6 Get them to do as much of the setting up work within the workshop itself as possible, i.e. setting the time frame, outcomes, first steps, commitment to and diarized meeting dates, etc. This gives them every chance of getting the project underway before 'life' hits them again.

You could include those criteria within your Welcome Pack (see pp. 76–82) if you wanted to get them thinking about applications in advance and even assign them project teams if applicable and ask them to meet before the session to agree their area of focus.

That will mean each exercise and activity will be filtered according to its usefulness to their project, so you might have to manage their expectations during the overview if some of them are more generalized but still relevant to a bigger picture.

On the whole I strongly recommend projects – however 'mini' – as a highly effective way of aiding implementation of your subject back in the 'real world' and, in my experience, if they are set up well (interesting, relevant, well supported by line management), even the larger ones are enthusiastically carried out and enjoyed by the participants.

In addition, with any training or coaching intervention, it serves as a very tangible way of measuring return on investment and increases the time over which your participants interact with the material, which at the very least improves retention.

Project examples

- *Giving customers the 'Wow Factor'* – a three-week project following a two-day workshop with cross-functional teams applying the learning to customer satisfaction, resulting in several innovative and effective ideas (Welcome Pack, improved internal communications process, accelerated induction training). The groups returned for a half-day presentation of their worked-up idea and a 'winner' was chosen (though all ideas were eventually implemented).

- *Using evaluation proactively* – a two-week project after a one-day workshop where participants put together ideas for harnessing the 'market research' aspect of evaluation, followed up via an e-mail group a fortnight later where ideas, successes and suggestions were shared.

- *Innovating in engineering* – a six-week project of intradepartmental teams solving business issues in a large engineering company. Each team took on a company-wide problem and came up with suggestions for solving/improving it,

▶

presented back to the MD, who then gave feedback and steered them to the next step of implementation.

- *Motivating stressed staff* – a one-month (that became ongoing) project where participants of a motivation and communication skills workshop found small daily ways to implement the various approaches and tools they'd learned, incorporating progress reports and feedback/success sharing into their weekly team meetings.

Ways to follow up

So, you've designed and run the workshop and the project, whether large or mini, is under way – how do you ensure they've completed it?

This particularly applies if you haven't set up a project of any kind – follow-through will still ensure some application of learning. It's a deadline for the participants to work to and a way of getting feedback and a sense of completion.

You can follow through in a variety of ways:

- **One-to-one coaching** (you can reinforce, build and tailor the learning).

- **Telecoaching** (same again; best for non-physical skills and/or knowledge).

- **Teleclasses** (telecoaching in a group).[3]

- **E-mail or e-group** (least effective, but still some kind of check-in; best used with another medium).

- **Group session/coaching** (you all meet back and share outcomes/successes).

- **Presentation** (they present their project outcomes to you or another stakeholder).

- **Award ceremony** (where you or a stakeholder present them with an award for completing their project).

[3] For training on leading teleclasses, see www.coachu.com.

WHAT TYPE OF SESSION?

Workshop, seminar, taster or coaching group? There are horses for courses (if you'll excuse the pun). Figure 1.3 gives you a rough idea of the most commonly run types of session and why you might choose that format.

Figure 1.3 Session formats

Type of session	Time frame	No. of participants	When to use/comments*
Briefing	1–2 hrs	Varies, usually a team	To disseminate information, policy, strategy or process to a (usually functional) team; often a one-way process but potential for improved effectiveness through interactivity; process-oriented
Taster/Teaser	1–2 hrs	Varies	As an intro to a full workshop or course; to test out new ideas; to promote a course or event; as a 'learning byte' for busy people; results-oriented
Support group/ Therapy group	½–1 day	Usually no more than 12ish	To work through emotional or therapeutic issues in a safe environment; usually a closed group once set up in order to build safety and trust; informal facilitation style works best; process-oriented
Co-coaching group/Action learning set	1 hr–½ day	Usually small, up to 6–8	To maintain momentum once initial learning is set up (e.g. after a workshop); to disseminate skills in the workplace without the need for formal training; to promote self-responsibility and solution-oriented working; generally not or very loosely facilitated after set-up; process- and results-oriented
Meeting	1–2 hrs	Varies	To disseminate and share progress, information, knowledge and/or skills; to discuss (and ideally reach agreement on) a single or variety of topics; to react to immediate issues; can be facilitated by anyone present; often ongoing; process- and results-oriented, but often hampered by process

▶

Figure 1.3 continued

Type of session	Time frame	No. of participants	When to use/comments*
Group coaching	2 hrs–½ day	4 to 12ish	To solve or work on specific issues or ideas; usually highly task-focused sessions; can be ongoing or ad hoc; usually facilitated (co-coaching group if self-directed); results-oriented
Workshop	½–1 day, or more than 1 day (then 'course' or 'programme')	6 to 16	To disseminate skills and knowledge; often facilitated by someone experienced in said skills and application; can be focused on specific tasks or issues; usually a mixture of diverse activities during the session; results-oriented
Seminar	1–3 hours	Up to 20 or 30ish	To disseminate knowledge and information; usually led by 'expert' in subject; often process- and/or task-oriented
Presentation	5 mins–½ hr	Varies	To disseminate information; usually led by one person sharing the information to a group with invested interest; mostly used to promote self, ideas, products or services; results-oriented
Lecture	30 mins–2 hrs	Varies, up to 100s	Used to disseminate knowledge and information; usually led by 'expert' in subject; model is teaching v. training, so passive learning; process-oriented
Teleclass	30–90 mins	Varies, up to 100+	To disseminate or share information and knowledge; share verbal skills; as ongoing support to face-to-face sessions; to promote face-to-face sessions or telecourses

Note: * Explanation of process v. results-oriented.

● Process-oriented – the main focus is on the mode of delivery, whether deliberately as part of the outcome (e.g. action learning sets, group therapy) or because it is hard to ascertain the results at the time (e.g. lectures).

● Results-oriented – the focus is on the results or outcome, e.g. workshops (skills learned and practised), presentations (sale achieved or interview passed), group coaching (issue solved or ideas generated).

One or many?

Another thing to consider is whether a one-off session is really what you want to offer or your session would be better run as a short series of events – perhaps even via an alternative medium, such as a teleclass.

One common temptation when planning your first workshops is to cram too much into them, thereby depriving your participants of the opportunity to dip out of work or life and really get on board some useful concepts and/or skills.

Never underestimate the value of simply giving people the time away from their day-to-day responsibilities in order to take time out to consider their life or work; the space you create within the workshop and the opportunities you give your group to apply what you're sharing with them may sometimes be the only chance they get in the near future to use the material.

Hence, it might be of more value and contribution if you offer a number of shorter sessions than if you offer only two. For example, you could divide a one-day workshop into four evening, breakfast or lunchtime events that are not only easier to slot into a busy week but also spread the learning over a longer time, giving each person more chances to try out the learning for themselves and build on it bit by bit.

Offer them more

If you're offering more than one session, consider presenting them as a series or some kind of coded or numbered grouping that suggests – or, better still, states – that benefit will be gained from taking up more.

If you're a manager, this can be useful when designing workshops to enhance skills in that you can either divide one main topic into linked smaller ones that build on each other, facilitating the skills transfer more easily back at work, or, if you have several topics to deliver, packaging them in this way helps you create links that either encourages uptake or reinforces learning. If you're an external facilitator, this has obvious implications for upselling and cross-selling.

For example, you have three interesting workshops, each standalone and on offer to a variety of audiences. Finding a way of linking and sequencing them so that logically they connect and build on one another allows you to offer them as a programme of modules that still can be taken separately, but which implies that greater benefit is conferred by completing the whole programme.

You can present this in a variety of ways, for example:

- gold, silver, bronze levels;

- colour-coded programmes, themed by audience, sub-topic, skill level, etc.;

- numbered modules;

- symbols indicating audience, sub-topic, skill level, etc.;

- upgrading to a value-added package which includes additional products/services; or

- discounts or other incentives if more than one module is booked at one time.

The overall message is: why stop at one session?

YOUR PARTICIPANTS

Briefly, what do you know about your participants? Whether you're a manager running this session inhouse or an independent facilitator running an open session, it's worth spending a few minutes thinking about your potential audience.

Participant profile

- Who are your participants? If you've absolute freedom in deciding whom to invite, who are your *ideal* participants?

- What are they interested in, other than your session subject?

- What do they want to achieve, gain, have more of?

- What are their common problems? What do they want less of, to avoid, to prevent?

- Why do you think they're coming to your session? Were they sent or have they chosen to come?

- What else could they get from attending that would add even greater value to their experience?

Overcoming resistance

One of the situations you might find yourself up against at some point is a roomful of people who, frankly – and sometimes openly – just don't want to be there. This could be because they've been sent as part of their development or it's a company-wide series of briefings about a subject as exciting as drying paint.

Rather than wading through the mud of open or implied resentment, what you want is a way of allaying fears or expected boredom and getting them into a frame of mind that, if not exactly enthusiastic, is at least open.

You've weeded out and spring-cleaned your own beliefs about the session and the participants, but what about them? You can't control their assumptions, can you?

Well, 'control' maybe not – but you can certainly influence. Before they even have contact with you (and if it's your team, even if they have daily contact with you), you can certainly *influence* the way they think of the session they're to attend. In fact, I would tentatively suggest that the more assumptions they're likely to have about your session, the more important it is for you to go about influencing them positively.

How can you do this? In a variety of ways before, during and after your session.

Before

The simplest way is by using a Welcome Pack – targeted contact with them before the session. Pages 76–82 cover this in detail, but, in short, it's an opportunity for you to set up and/or confound your participants' expectations, 'warm them up' and even begin the learning.

Even if you've hardly any time beforehand or don't have the resources to send a physical pack, a well-aimed e-mail is still worth the effort. Aim to:

- sound genuinely welcoming;

- set them a task, question or puzzle;

- get some kind of response from them prior to their arrival if possible;

- set realistic expectations and add a hint of other things to come.

During

Worst case scenario: you're in front of a group of people and you know (sometimes by being told in no uncertain terms) that they don't want to be there. What do you do? Acknowledge it.

The fact is, they *are* there – and so are you. From that point, you can all choose to use the precious time to get something genuinely useful out of the session or doggedly insist on wasting it (and therefore that number of hours of their lives) by refusing to engage.

Setting up that choice in a light-hearted way is often all you need to do to get them, even grudgingly, willing to participate on some level . . . and the rest will be done by your design, since they'll be so engaged in the material that they'll have forgotten they didn't want to be there within half an hour or so.

After

Even if you've had a dire session and are glad the last person's out of the room (hopefully highly unlikely if you apply the design principles in this book), you can still salvage something.

Follow-up of any kind is always useful and whether that's a check-in call, formal coaching session, group meeting or even an e-mail, it's a chance to boost learning, shape memories, leave a 'nice taste' and ensure use of the new knowledge. Pages 14–18 covered ways to do this and, if all else has failed, it can be a very effective way to mend bridges and sweeten a less than positive experience on both sides.

Blending into their culture

If you're an external provider working with a group then useful general information would include anything about the group's shared background, industry or culture. Not so that you can bone up on it and try to come across as knowledgeable in their field (a very dangerous game if you're not genuinely from that background), but so that you can choose your explanations to suit the group – which often has the same effect.

For example, using dance as a way of describing the complexity of communication with a group of engineers might not be the most effective way to get them on board with your ideas and imagining themselves using the skills you're so generously sharing (unless, of course, you really strike lucky and find that they're members of a ballet school in their spare time) . . . but likening it to smoothly running cogs and wheels in a larger machine is at least attempting a closer match with their day-to-day culture.

This simple device of explaining concepts and skills by using analogies that are from or in sympathy with their own industry can be a powerful way of overcoming the 'You're not from round here, are you?' syndrome and set of beliefs that it encompasses.

Group size

Something that will also have an impact on design choices is number of participants. You may already have an idea about this after deciding on the style of session you'd like to run, but sometimes the number is dictated to us or is suddenly changed.

Figure 1.4 shows the design implications for varying numbers in terms of how they can affect the natural style of a session.

Figure 1.4 The effect of group size on the choice of session format

Number	Design implications
6 or fewer	Not really a 'workshop' or similar; the style would be even more informal than a workshop, with the facilitator probably sitting mostly with the group – best suited to group coaching if you're running it
7 to 16ish	This number is perfect for most workshops and allows one-to-one contact with everyone during the session to ensure they're 'getting it'; facilitator up front and with group during exercises
17 to 30ish (large workshop/ seminar)	Acceptable as a large workshop if there is more than one facilitator, lots of space and very well structured and not essential to have one-to-one contact with all in each session – for example, a longer programme or a knowledge- rather than skills-based subject; facilitator would need to be up front in order to reach the group clearly, but still working among the group during exercises
31 to 60ish (seminar)	Though many seminars have smaller groups, interactivity may be reduced at this size compared with a workshop. Seminar if individual contact time is not important in the session; facilitator up front mostly
60 upwards (large seminar/ lecture or conference)	Again, lectures can of course be given to smaller numbers, but at this size interactivity is usually even less than a seminar and very little individual attention given. Clever combinations of up-front explanations and interactive audience exercises can help this

By now you should have a pretty good idea where your session sits in terms of size, intent and potential for interactivity.

LOCATION, LOCATION, LOCATION

Whether a boardroom with an immovable table, a lecture theatre or a converted warehouse, the venue (particularly if outside your control) can have ramifications on your design; therefore, it's one of the earliest things to get sorted out.

The ideal room

An ideal room would comprise the following.

● **Natural lighting** – almost essential for sessions longer than a couple of hours.

- **Lots of floor space** – ideally as much floor space again as there is occupied by seated areas (including tables).

- **Ability to move tables around** (some are fixed, too heavy or too large to offer positioning flexibility).

- **Round tables** if using cabaret style (my personal layout of choice for an interactive session).

- **Proximity to outdoors**, public space (e.g. large hotel lobby) or break-out rooms.

You will need access to the room at least an hour before the session (more if it's a particularly complex set-up), so ensure you're not running your session back to back with another group. (See 'Setting the scene', pp. 144–54, for detailed guidelines on setting up a room.)

Solutions to non-ideal rooms

If for whatever reason you get landed with a non-ideal room, here are some workarounds to the commonest issues.

No natural lighting

- Use break-out rooms or other outside space if it's a long session.

- Incorporate 'walkabout' energizing exercises that get people out and into natural light for short bursts.

- Keep each section short (no more than 30–40 minutes) with plenty of out-of-room energy or 'natural' breaks.

No or very little floor space or opportunities for movement

- Do BrainGym (see pp. 94–9) while standing by/behind their chairs.

- Get people to swap seats for various exercises.

- Move chairs around into small groups for certain exercises (dependent on space).

- Get them out of the room on walkabouts.

- Vary styles of exercises to stimulate and change energy in room.

Fixed tables/boardroom layout

- Group people in teams according to sides of table to emulate the grouping of a cabaret-style room.

- Change ends of table/walk around yourself (if room) to avoid 'top table' syndrome with facilitator over-represented and creating a 'them/us' feel.

- Use table interactively – toys, games, flowcharts, timelines on lengths of brown paper, games, building 3D models of processes/concepts to discuss, etc.

Square or too-large tables in cabaret style

- Group around three sides of table rather than four if too large.

- Square tables, even if right size, can mean some people have their back to you when presenting, so vary your position and walk around the room, using different areas to present different topics or aspects (see also 'Intelligent space', pp. 146–150).

Different room styles

When using an external venue provider, it's as well to be au fait with the shorthand used to describe different room layouts when you're discussing your requirements. Figure 1.5 details the main styles.

Figure 1.5 Main room styles

Style/layout	Description	Uses	Comments
Circle	Participants and facilitator sit in circle; no physical 'head' of group	Highly informal arrangement well suited to therapy and co-coaching groups where there is no obvious leader. Very flexible in terms of movement	Can feel a bit 'touchy-feely' for business/skills workshop layouts unless the set-up is for a pragmatic exercise. Emphasizes the 'equality' of everyone
Horseshoe	Participants sit in horseshoe arrangement, facilitator in gap at	Informal arrangement for group coaching, soft skills workshops, some therapy groups	No desks for leaning on/writing, so not suitable for long periods of delivery or note-taking

▶

Figure 1.5 continued

Style/layout	Description	Uses	Comments
	the top facing them	Very flexible in terms of movement	
Cabaret	Small tables dotted around a larger room with up to 6 seats at each Facilitator anywhere in room; not necessarily 'anchored' to head or any visual aids	Semi-formal arrangement well suited to workshops depending on size of room and numbers Very flexible for movement of facilitator and/or participants Desks provide support for writing and team-focused activities My room layout of choice for workshops	Large numbers in large rooms (>30) can present visual access issues unless using PowerPoint at one or more ends
Boardroom	Usually up to 20, chairs placed around a central large table	Fairly formal layout depending on size of group/table Commonly used for meetings Doesn't lend itself to much flexibility, particularly if also in a room with restricted space Chair or facilitator usually sits at table head	Table can be used as a 'board' for interactive games or used as 'wallspace' to introduce greater interactivity
Classroom	Participants seated at desks all facing same way, often in rows Facilitator at front with visual aid(s)	Formal arrangement best suited to seminars and lectures Conveys a 'school' feel and may have unhelpful associations for some people Very inflexible space for movement	Even if necessary for technical reasons (e.g. computer training), theming the room/desks can alleviate associations and create more positive expectations
Lecture or theatre style	Chairs only, all facing towards the front in rows Sometimes a gradient from back down to front so that all can see the front clearly Often a lectern/podium for presenter	Very formal arrangement best suited to lectures and formal long presentations Very inflexible space	Interactivity can be introduced through participants discussing in pairs and small groups Parts of the room could be divided into 'teams' for informal research exercises – even by show of hands 'Mexican wave' or similar to keep energy up

INFORMATION V. LEARNING

To save you both time and effort, before getting started with the design proper you might first want to consider how much of what you intend to go into the session is pure information, by which I mean anything that could ordinarily be given out in written form or put up on PowerPoint or overhead transparencies, such as policies, procedures, theory, etc.

The good news is that there are quicker, easier and more effective ways of getting information-heavy content over than delivering it point-by-point.

Which is which?

So what exactly *is* information, and what *is* learning? A simple test is to look at your content (especially the theory-heavy parts or parts that would ordinarily be handed out, put up on slides or read out) and ask yourself which parts could the participants do.

- read for themselves? (*Information*)
- find out for themselves? (*Learning*)
- draw from their own experience? (*Learning*)
- find out from each other? (*Learning*)
- research and feed back to you/each other? (*Learning*)

The only passive learning in the above five categories is 'read for themselves' (and even that doesn't mean being read to, for example from a slide or handout), but using these combined approaches is actually how I handled a huge manual of over 300 pages of information that had previously been primarily talked through or shown as overhead transparencies (OHTs) as the teaching method. Needless to say, recall had been pretty low, as it took a whole week to get through the material. The manual ended up as a themed, interactive, game-ridden three-day romp, and recall went from around 25 per cent to consistently 80+ per cent.

A great deal of material that could easily be fitted into those categories is considered *information*, and therefore handed out, read to or lectured at participants, when really it would be a hop, skip and a jump to turn it into engaging activities that would lodge far more securely in the memory if allowed to enter dynamically instead of passively.

A common objection to turning theory-based information into more dynamic learning is that it's 'legislation', or 'procedure', and has to be imparted just as it is. I agree; it does. But where does it state that it has to be imparted in such a turgid, passive, dull way that you are almost guaranteed a 90 per cent amnesia rate?

Converting 'serious' subjects from delivery as handouts, OHTs, Power-Point slides or sitting round and talking through each page into interactive games, exercises, flowcharts and models does not detract from the importance of the material or trivialize it. Rather, it brings it to life and helps it make the connections it needs in the brain to find a permanent home there.

In order for something to be remembered beyond the next few minutes it has to be repeated, and it also has to find associations in the brain on which to 'hang' itself. This is one of the reasons why the more abstract subjects at school such as algebra are harder to remember; unless you were planning to use it in your career (lots of connections and associations), there was nothing to hang the formulae on that related to your own life or experiences and therefore the information was left somewhere on the 'Misc' pile of your cerebral desk. And we all know how easy it is to remember what's even in a 'Misc' pile, much less find a specific item there.

So – your mission, should you choose to accept it, is to take a look at what you are planning to include in your session (headings/subheads) and, with your participants in mind, sort it into the four categories outlined in Figure 1.6.

A word about the four categories.

- **Before you see them** – the faster they can be engaged, the greater the learning and the more 'warmed up' to your subject they will be when they arrive.

- **What's already in them** – personal experience is a 'ready-made hook' for the information and people often already know a lot more

Figure 1.6 Turning information into learning

Before you see them (outside session) *What can they read, do or find out before they even walk through the door?*	What's already in them (inside/outside session) *What can they draw from their own experience or that of others through contact or discussion?*
Active learning (inside session) *What can they find out as an active game, puzzle, hunt or active research as part of the session?*	Active teaching (inside session) *Could they assimilate and teach back the information creatively instead of you?*

than they think if you can draw it out. Also, find as many ways as you can to get them to link what they're learning to their own lives, even if bizarrely – it still works!

- **Active learning** – actively discovering information stays far longer in the memory than being told or shown as it involves far more neural pathways and often both sides of the brain.

- **Active teaching** – this is double learning in that they have to 'know' their subject before they teach it, then they teach it. You stand by as a coach for their preparation and during the teachback to ensure all points are covered clearly.

Passive learning

I would respectfully suggest that there is no place for passive teaching in a workshop or interactive session in the form of 'Here is a handout; this is what it says' or 'Here is a slide; this is what it says'. Unless you're teaching adult literacy or English as a foreign language, everyone can read – allow them to do that either interactively or in their own time.

Information made easy

But what if you do have chunks of information that you have to get across, yet with the best will in the world you haven't the time to turn them into puzzles or activities? What if you're a manager tasked with briefing your team with changes to the latest policies or maybe a consultant having to get across some important but less-than-exciting aspect of a management operating system?

Well, there are still many ways to present information without having to resort to showing (on slides, OHTs, etc.) and talking it through.

Send it

Rather than talking it through passively, why not send the information to your participants before they even get to you so that your time with them is focused more on clarifying any aspects they're not sure of or getting it further into their memories?

'But they won't read it!' you cry. They will if there's a good reason to – and by 'good', I mean interesting or rewarding. For example, you could:

- attach a set of questions to be answered and brought;
- set a task related to the contents that they complete for the workshop/briefing session;
- advise them that the first activity of the session is a quiz on the information;
- ask each participant to come with three questions or, alternatively three points that they consider relevant to raise in the group.

This way you're extending the contact time with you, getting them involved in the subject before the day of the event, extending their learning time and doing some of the work before the day, leaving you freed up for more hands-on activities and time to facilitate their applying the learning.

Hide it

Another way to convey information is to hide it . . . around the room, inside each other (give different participants 'slices' of information and get them to put them all together through interviewing each other and sharing it), in different parts of the building. We never grow out of treasure hunts, so if you've time to set up clues, too, so much the better!

This makes the learning more fun and active – information can be dry and hard to concentrate on, so setting it within an activity that involves hunting it down adds zest and energy to it.

Request it

If the information can be found somewhere on the web, in a library, inhouse . . . ask them to get it for you and present it back to each other. This can be set as a pre-session task or done during the workshop. That way you can help them build the presentation and fill in any gaps in their research.

The only caveat to this approach is that, if groups or individuals are presenting information to each other as a teaching method, there needs to be an added incentive to concentrate on the content of each others' presentations – such as a later quiz, for example – since otherwise they will be easily distracted by thoughts about their own presentation.

Display it

Rather than simply handing out sheets of information or talking them through, why not post them on a set of boards on the wall in a gallery style? This way you can walk through them like an art gallery or get people to do a walkaround of the information, finding answers to a set of questions handed to them on arrival. This is a much more informal way of getting over points.

To help ensure that they take in the information you could add a quiz or similar exercise (info bingo, etc.) later in the session. You can always give them a set of the notes to take home.

2

CHAPTER TWO
Whole-brain learning primer

You should by now have an idea of your style, type of session and general and personal outcomes. This next section is both an overview of whole-brain learning and a source of instantly usable tips and ideas for your session.

This will give you all the knowledge you need to start creating interactive exercises of your own, but a host of off-the-shelf activities can be found in Chapter 3 ('Building a great session') if you'd prefer to tailor tried-and-tested activities.

THE BIGGEST MYTH IN TRAINING

One of the first questions I usually get asked when training people in interactive facilitation skills and workshop design – particularly if they're used to a style of presenting that is heavily reliant upon PowerPoint and overhead projectors – is:

Won't I lose control of the group?

There is an understandable concern that, by shifting perceived 'control' away from the presenter towards the group in the form of group activities and participant-led learning, the activity – or even the session itself – could somehow run away from them.

Hand on heart, I have never seen this happen. In fact, the very opposite applies: it's actually easier to keep 'control' of the group when in more facilitative mode (provided, of course, it's a well-designed session), for the following reasons:

- the group is far more engaged in their task, activity or learning than they would be sitting passively listening;

- you automatically have their attention occupied, so, instead of having to work hard to make your slides, overhead transparencies or anecdotes interesting enough to keep it, all you need to do is channel it;

- your participants can gain immediate results – whether by completing a task, discovering something new or applying knowledge to their situation – rather than having a 'time lag' between receiving new information and applying it;

- by appealing to 'multiple channels' (i.e. more than just their eyes and ears), you automatically involve more cerebral capacity – leaving less to 'wander';

- it is far easier to feel and appear knowledgeable when dropping in on working groups and offering advice and guidance than having to know all the answers up front;

- finally, it is far, far easier to get a group interacting, talking to you and asking questions during whole-group discussions or debriefs if they've just spent the last 20 minutes in that mode, rather than expecting them to chat away after 20 minutes of sitting in silence listening to you talk.

So, if losing control is a concern of yours, fear not: you'll actually gain more of it.

ALL YOU NEED TO KNOW ABOUT LEARNING THEORY

This is a bold statement, I know, but unless you're a trainer I consider the following whistlestop tour of learning to be all the bare essentials of learning theory you'll need to know in order to create really effective, interactive and memorable workshops and group sessions of any kind.

The two models of learning that I consider indispensable when designing and running a workshop are:

- the four main precepts of whole-brain learning theory;

- Honey and Mumford's four learning styles.

Whether creating your own exercises or deciding which ones to include, understanding these models will ensure you get a good balance of activities that should suit all learning styles and play to everyone's strengths.

The four main precepts of whole-brain learning theory

Whole-brain learning is a process that engages far more of the brain than conventional methods of teaching and training, which rely heavily on left-brain (logical, linguistic) processing, a more passive model of learning (lecture, presentations) and don't engage all of the senses. There are many excellent books on the subject and if you're planning to become a trainer or are interested in delving fully into this area, I've recommended my favourites in the Resources section at the end of the book.

In contrast to traditional, or left-brain, learning, whole-brain learning by definition is all about using both sides of the brain, so the process is more creative; it actively involves the participants in the learning through discovery, creation and exploration of the material; and it engages the body and as many of the senses as possible in as many ways as possible.

Whole-brain learning helps participants:

- retain information longer;

- recall information easier;

- take in new information faster; and

- enjoy the learning process more.

The downside that often isn't mentioned is that, from a facilitator's point of view, sessions can take longer to design as there's more creation involved up front. However, they will be far more enjoyable to run and far better received by your participants than a 'chalk and talk' session would be, and as well as the benefits to the participants, there are additional benefits to you:

- greater 'control' of the group;

- happier, more engaged participants;

- more comfortable facilitation – the onus isn't 100 per cent on you to 'deliver', it's shared;

- more chance to boost implementation through coaching;

- huge flexibility and endless options – if one thing doesn't work, you'll always have another 50 up your sleeve;

- more fun, for you and your participants – once tried, people rarely go back to conventional delivery.

These are the fundamentals of whole-brain theory that I find most pertinent to workshop design.

1 Engage both halves of the brain: left, or logical/linear/linguistic, together with right, or creative/musical/holistic.

2 Use 'multi-channel' learning so that the body and brain are engaged as much as possible: reason, sound/speech, vision, physical movement, even smell and taste where you can.

3 We have multiple intelligences, not just two, so involve as many as you can.

4 Having fun allows people to learn faster and retain information longer, so feel free to enjoy yourselves – use games, themes, toys, upbeat activities . . .

Note: Whole-brain learning doesn't require that the participants are *continually* active and that *everything* must be turned into a game, discovery or creation. Like all natural entities, the brain has a rhythm, too, so it is perfectly acceptable to punctuate interactive periods with some more passive activities, such as facilitator delivery, journaling or other more reflective time, in order to give your participants a chance to assimilate and categorize what they've just learned. I have seen people go from one extreme to the other in delivery style!

1 Using 'both brains'

As can be seen from Figure 2.1, we have two halves to our brains, each with distinct strengths and faculties.

Unless working in the creative industries, in the workplace we mostly favour a 'left-brain' way of working:

- logic over intuition;
- linear over lateral;
- monochrome over multicolour;
- words and/or figures over pictures or symbols.

Figure 2.1 Left and right hemispheres of the brain

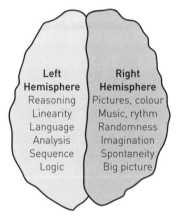

While this mostly works very well, ignoring the right side of our brains means we fail to tap into a huge potential source of creativity, ideas and connections that the more logical left side might not offer.

There are many easy ways of encouraging the use of both sides of the brain when conducting workshops.

- **Colour** – in visuals, around the room, by colour-coding subjects, objects on tables, tablecloths.

- **Music** – as background, welcome, with energizers, in breaks, as themes (see pp. 48–51 for more on this).

- **Mindmaps** – to teach and for taking notes.

- **Pictures** – whether graphs or symbols, flowcharts or posters, use pictures as well as words in your visuals as a good picture can convey hundreds of words.

- **The overview** – the right brain makes connections and prefers to see things holistically, so make sure you give the overview before going into detail.

- **Imagination** – get your participants to create in their mind what it will be like to have achieved their outcomes or be applying the skills using all their senses.

- **Play** – there is a close association between play and learning, especially if the emotions and humour are involved, so don't be afraid to get your participants to do 'silly' things such as warm-ups or as exercises with learning outcomes attached.

How could you involve the right brain more in your session?

2 Using 'multi-channel' learning

You've probably gathered by now that I consider interactive sessions – whether workshops, seminars, meetings or group coaching – to be better than passive ones.

How many of these would be useful to you?

❏ Your participants learn quickly.

❏ Information you share with them is retained.

❏ Your participants can shift what they learn from you from short- to long-term memory easily.

❏ The information and skills you share are applied to your participants' work/lives.

❏ Your group enjoys the session hugely.

❏ Group energy is maintained throughout the session – even after lunch!

All of these are far more likely when you use multiple channels to convey your information, skills or knowledge to your group.

So, cutting to the chase, you need to involve four things during your session (where possible within each exercise): reasoning, sound, vision and physicality (see Figure 2.2).

Figure 2.2 The four elements of multi-channel learning

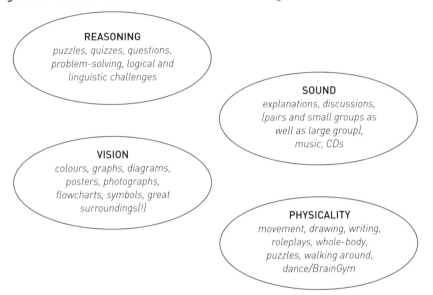

Using multiple channels for design

Most traditional training and presentation styles lean heavily on one or two channels across which to deliver their information: usually the auditory (lecturing, discussion) and visual (PowerPoint slides, OHTs, flipcharts). However colourful the slides and interesting the speaker, this still leaves out two very powerful channels through which to convey the message: physicality and reasoning. While involving reasoning often plays to the left brain (conundrums, problems, puzzles, questions, tasks) and so is more easily added in, the body as a learning channel is often overlooked.

The added advantage of using physical means to transfer information and learning is that not only does it improve uptake of the information and speed the learning process but it also:

- energizes the body and therefore person, increasing concentration times;

- changes the person's emotional state, which is useful for when discussions get stuck or debates get heated;

- improves blood flow around the body, increasing oxygen supply to the brain;

- usually involves both sides of the brain, increasing cerebral involvement and therefore boosting learning potential.

So for speed-designing, make sure your activities use **RSVP**:

- **Reasoning** (intellectual challenges, quizzes, puzzles, real-life problems, conundrums, tests, pre-session tasks, paradoxes, quests, structured exercises);

- **Sound** (discussions in pairs, groups, presentations, CDs, musical background and accompaniment, notes, rhymes/raps, jingles, interviews, lectures and mini-lectures, press conferences, telecoaching or teleclasses, stories);

- **Vision** (colours, shape, environment, posters, visualization, textbooks and workbooks, cards, badges, crosswords, written stories, diagrams and flowcharts, graphs, symbols, colour-coding or theming);

- **Physicality** (movement, changing position, games, floor puzzles/physical puzzles, walkabouts to find things, being in nature, breathing exercises, acting out different scenarios changing seats, building things, using the hands, BrainGym).

3 Multiple intelligences in a nutshell

In addition to the mathematical/logical and linguistic intelligences tested in the traditional IQ test, we all have another six intelligences at least – and more are being 'discovered' all the time (Gardner, 1999).

The relevance of this for you is that the more you include multisensory, multi-channel activities in your workshops, the more you'll play to everyone in your audience's strengths, not just the more 'academic' types.

This will lead to more effective and successful workshops and better implementation of the learning – and, of course, a great reputation for you.

As an overview, here are the main eight intelligences.

Linguistic

Characteristics: At home with words in any form, loves language and wordplay, stories, rhymes, writing.

Ideas for exercises: Have participants create rhymes, raps or puns, tell stories, play word games (e.g. crosswords, quizzes), write notes, use learning journals.

Mathematical/logical

Characteristics: Likes problem solving, applies logic easily, enjoys working with numbers, good at recognizing patterns.

Ideas for exercises: Create flowcharts of processes, storyboards, checklists, set problems to be analysed and solved, use logic puzzles, create sets and groups.

Visual/spatial

Characteristics: Creates mental images, good at translating what is seen into pictures, thinks three-dimensionally, can judge relationships between objects accurately.

Ideas for exercises: Paint or draw posters/pictures of concepts being learned, use mindmaps, use DVDs and videos, colour-code subjects, construct 3D models.

Musical

Characteristics: Can sing or play an instrument, able to recognize and/or carry a tune, enjoys moving to a beat, aware of patterns in sounds.

Ideas for exercises: Get participants to create a rap or song of the learning using a well-known tune, use music throughout the session, musical energy breaks.

Interpersonal

Characteristics: Sensitive to feelings and moods of others, and to non-verbal communication, good at building rapport and interacting with people.

Ideas for exercises: Create team competitions or quizzes, have participants contact each other before the session and/or work together afterwards, teach each other, use buddying and co-coaching during projects.

Intrapersonal

Characteristics: Very self-aware, interested in personal development, likes to meditate and spend time alone, happy to work independently of others.

Ideas for exercises: Set up a learning journal, use observational skills for coaching, give opportunities for reflective time, use guided imagery/meditations.

Physical

Characteristics: Moves about a lot, uses body to both communicate and work out problems (e.g. pacing), usually sporty or highly active, often has physical hobbies.

Ideas for exercises: Any physical activities, BrainGym, plays or acting out, use props to illustrate points and for participants to play with, plenty of energy breaks.

Naturalist

Characteristics: At home in nature, whether with animals or just outdoors, environmentally aware, concerned about sustainability and social impact.

Ideas for exercises: Allow access to outdoors where possible, use plenty of nature-based symbols and metaphor, have fresh flowers/plants in the room, natural light.

4 Have fun

Have you ever been in a workshop when, at the beginning, 'Have fun' was set as part of the ground rules? Then nobody did? While you can't force people to have fun on command or demand, you certainly can design your workshop in a way that they're likely to, *without* it having to be set in ground rules (but see also my comments on ground rules, pp. 90–1).

There is a perfectly scientific reason for fun – or at least light-hearted enjoyment – being an important part of workshop design: recall of information is significantly improved when emotions – positive or negative – are involved.

Think about a particular lesson from school that has stuck in your mind, or maybe a teacher. What is it about them you remember? Did you really enjoy the lesson with them? Was that particular lesson a high – or low – point in your schooldays? What were the highlights of your schooldays? Whether negative or positive, emotions aid memory.

Of course, it goes without saying that you want your participants to remember your sessions for the *right* reasons. Therefore, it's best to design with positive emotions in mind – and games, fun, humour, light-heartedness and creativity all facilitate this. Themes are a great way of incorporating all of the above, while also being a powerful learning vehicle themselves when well-chosen.

Honey and Mumford's four learning styles

In the 1970s, Peter Honey and Alan Mumford (see the Resources section at the end of the book for their website) proposed a model of learning styles that still remains one of the most useful when designing interactive sessions – and particularly now that whole-brain learning is coming to the forefront.

Your own learning style will heavily influence your design and natural facilitation style so do have a quick read through the four types so you can decide which apply most to you.

Activist

People who fall into this learning preference like to learn by doing. They are often quite proactive and have short attention spans and will be very frustrated by long periods of passive learning, such as lengthy explanations, PowerPoint or other visual and non-active presentations, etc.

They respond best when given an exercise that involves action – whether that be a puzzle to solve, treasure hunt, even something to make or draw – and other people. Once they have grasped a skill or piece of knowledge they'll want to move on to the next, so a slower-paced style of delivery will tend to frustrate them. When including downtime in the session, give the participants the option to go somewhere else to reflect so that the activists can get moving again.

Pragmatist

These people like to know the 'why' of any learning – they don't respond well to 'I'll explain later's or abstract exercises designed to teach a concept that isn't immediately and obviously related to their work or life.

Pragmatists respond best to some explanation up front about why this might be useful to them or their work – and if you really don't want to give away the 'punchline' for some reason before the exercise, simply let them know when that will become clear. They like exercises with obvious benefits and applications, so the debrief of any exercise is highly important, as this is when they will want to find out how to use that skill or knowledge if it wasn't apparent during the activity.

Reflector

Reflectors like to stand back and evaluate what they're taking in – for some that means overnight; for others, just a few minutes of quiet contemplation or note-writing. Often they will not form an opinion on something until they've had this time to think it through and place the material into context, so it can be useful if you need feedback on a concept, idea or proposal to ask for it before a long break (e.g. lunch) or send the proposal to them before the session and ask them to have formulated questions and/or thoughts before they attend.

It is possible to overload reflectors if your session is overly active and negatively affect their ability to learn, so ensure that levels of high activity are punctuated with breaks for people to pull together their thoughts and review what they've learned.

Theorist

These are the 'analysts' of your audience – they are the ones who want to know who, when, where and how, and like to have the option of checking out the facts for themselves. They'll appreciate clearly structured instructions, references, further reading, fact sheets, names and dates and they are not overloaded by text and notes – in fact, they could feel short-changed by insufficient reading material.

To keep these people happy without having to write a tome as your support materials, provide photocopied references of applications, reading lists (ideally with copies of some of the books in the room for them to thumb through) and, as a minimum, ensure that where possible you make references to other authorities, backed up with names and dates so that they can look them up themselves later if required. Make sure your instructions to activities are very clear and that debriefs are structured and comprehensive.

Design implications

I have seen a propensity (particularly if the facilitator is mainly activist) to overdo the 'active learning' whole-brain approach – for all the right reasons – and leave out reflectors and theorists through insufficient downtime and/or structure.

I'm an activist/pragmatist myself and therefore find that the four styles provide a useful way of reminding myself to include sufficient downtime, for my participants to catch their breath and consolidate the learning, and to be more structured in my approach. Otherwise, it can be too easy to create a non-stop active session that, while great fun for me and the other activists in the room, is too much input for the reflectors and too little information for the theorists.

What thoughts do you have for your own session?

USING MUSIC

There are many reasons for using music within a session of any kind, whether short seminar or day-long workshop. They include:

- energy and/or emotional management;
- changing focus;
- enhancing learning;
- aiding recall;
- signalling breaks or activities;
- creating a theme.

When and how to use it

Before the session

Why: Background music as people arrive helps to create a welcoming atmosphere and avoids what I call 'dentist's waiting room syndrome', where people sit in a self-conscious hush and speak in lowered tones or whispers.

What it does: In this case music acts as friendly 'white noise', allowing people to talk more freely and interact.

How to use it: If you are using a theme for your session, then the music could pick up on and introduce that; otherwise, use upbeat and 'feel-good' music at a low–moderate volume. Take care to choose music that can offend no one, even at the risk of being too 'easy listening' (jazz and blues are good choices).

What kinds of music could you use?

During the session

Why: While you are talking or when whole-group discussions are taking place, there should be no music. However, during exercises music can be used to good effect to:

- enhance concentration;

- raise energy;

- stimulate the right brain; and

- help recall and learning.

What it does: When using music in exercises, it helps in a variety of ways.

- For analytical or small group/pairs discussion exercises, using baroque music stimulates beta brainwaves, which aids concentration.

- For creative, energetic or team exercises, upbeat music stimulates the right brain and also helps raise energy. Again, if you have a theme, then use music related to that (TV/film themes, etc.).

- For review or reflective exercises, 'new age' music or slower movement classical music encourages alpha brainwaves, the ideal state for recall and learning.

How to use it: Generally choose non-vocals over vocal tunes as words can be disruptive to some people's thinking processes, but if the exercises are creative and fairly noisy then it's less of an issue. Volume moderate to fairly loud depending on the activity. There are compositions for 'accelerated learning' designed specifically for such purposes (a supplier can be found in the Resources section).

What kinds of music could you use?

In breaks

Why: For breaks, the same kind of music as you used to welcome the participants is fine. It can be used for two purposes:

- welcoming white noise in the same way as before the session;

- a 'call back' signal to let people know the session is about to start.

What it does: Allows people to chat freely without self-consciousness. It is far harder to break a silence than talk within white noise and people feel less 'overheard' when talking against background noise, even if it's not loud enough to mask their voices. The 'call back' signal works in the same way as using space to trigger useful responses – an association is made between that music and time for something new.

How to use it: Use a low to moderate volume and fade it out as you get ready to welcome them back. If using the music as a 'call back' signal, choose a particular piece and always put it on just before you call them back from an exercise or break. Let them know the first time what its purpose is so they know that when they hear it a new session is about to begin.

What kinds of music could you use?

At the end of the session

Why: It's a nice touch to play the participants out of the room on upbeat music – it's one of the ways in which you can use music as mood or energy enhancement.

What it does: Instead of simply filing out of a quiet room, specifically using a track to close the session makes the ending more deliberate, celebratory and brings it to a definite conclusion. It also creates another connection, this time emotional, to the session itself – chances are that when they hear that piece of music again they will recall the experience and hopefully some of the learning.

How to use it: You could use music related to a theme, repeat music used for a popular exercise or just go for 'feelgood' music – but make sure the lyrics are in keeping, as some fairly upbeat-sounding songs actually have fairly depressing lyrics.

What kinds of music could you use?

Caveat

Be careful about being overly personal in your choice and really think about the mood you want to create. One workshop I attended as a participant had Neil Diamond playing as the background music all lunchtime. Now while I personally love Neil Diamond, some of his songs aren't the happiest and, by the time we were ready to start the afternoon session, I was feeling *really* down, having listened to some of his saddest songs for over 20 minutes!

You can't avoid people's personal associations with songs, of course, but choosing upbeat songs at least suggests that the associations are more likely to be happy than sad. Classical music is usually safest of all, though, again, stick to the upbeat compositions other than using it for review sessions and reflective times and, even then, it's fairly clear what is a 'sad' composition and a 'restful' one. For example, it's probably best to avoid Barber's 'Adagio for Strings' (the *Platoon* theme) – though classical, the strings are powerfully used to evoke emotions of anguish and grief and, even if you haven't seen the film to have the visual images connected to it, the track alone can do this if you're sensitive to music.

ENERGY

A quick word about energy: it's worth keeping one eye on the 'temperature' of the room at all times to assess the level of energy. Too long on one exercise, or an activity that's long and passive, can drop the energy in the room, suppressing participants' willingness to contribute and even sending some people to sleep!

As a toe-in-the-water check, have a quick look at your day/session plan and ensure that your sections are different enough in nature to offer natural energy changes before adding in the breaks and any scheduled energy boosters. As you run the session itself you'll be able to tell whether you need additional ones, of course, but it's an idea to design the session from the outset with that in mind.

Here's a rough guide to the scale of low to high energy.

HIGH

Dance/BrainGym (see pp. 94–9)
Team physical games
Team craft/building/roleplay tasks
Competitive/team quizzes
Treasure hunts
Pairs/3s exercises
Walkabouts/information tours
Discussion groups/interviews
Writing/drawing (teams/pairs)
Facilitator-led explanation/presentation
Writing/drawing (individual)
Reading
Visualization/meditative exercises

LOW

Low-energy activities are not 'bad' – in fact they're needed by more reflective people – but they do need to be balanced by higher-energy activities in order to keep interest and concentration levels up . . . thereby maximizing the learning and retention of your well-designed content!

Think in terms of nature: there is a natural ebb and flow to all things, so include this natural rhythm in your session.

THE 70/30 RULE

No, not the 80/20 rule (though you could get away with that[1]).

According to Dave Meier, an excellent authority on whole-brain learning for trainers, the best balance between participant- and facilitator-led activities is 70/30.

Extrapolated (as is my wont), that means:

70% participant-oriented activities (i.e. exercises)

30% facilitator-oriented (i.e. delivery/presentation)

and/or

[1] Never less than 60/40.

70% high – medium energy activities/engagement

30% low-energy activities/reflection

and/or

70% learning

30% breaks/review

So far we've covered a wide range of tips and guidelines for creating your own whole-brain activities, but if you want to dip into some ready-made exercises, pp. 92–117 contain a variety that you can use or adapt.

BREAKS

Breaks come in a variety of flavours:

- refreshment breaks;
- lunch breaks;
- energy breaks;
- comfort breaks;
- review breaks.

The first two are fairly standard in most day-length workshops; the last three are less commonly seen.

Refreshment breaks

Time – usually 15 minutes.

Purpose – to punctuate a morning or afternoon section of activities/input or to end a session.

Comment – always provide 'healthy' alternatives such as water, juices, non-caffeinated hot drinks (herbal teas, etc.), fruit or non-sugary snacks as well as biscuits.

Lunch breaks

Time – usually anything from 30 to 90 minutes.

Purpose – to refuel; sometimes also to network, continue a team-based task or preparation for another task to be continued after lunch.

Comment – 30 minutes really is the absolute minimum and, in a day-long workshop, I would suggest 45 minutes to be the minimum. Remember when providing sandwiches that just about everyone can eat 'vegetarian' sandwiches (and always do), but only meat-eaters can eat meat ones, so if there are vegetarians in the group err on the side of 66 per cent vegetarian to 33 per cent meat or at the very least 50/50.

Energy breaks

Time – 5 to 10 minutes is usually enough.

Purpose – for times when energy is flagging in the room – either post-lunch or through working on a 'heavy' subject.

Comment – use BrainGym to upbeat music, 'silly' physical activities like teaching a dance move in teams, a review 'relay race' or other short physical review activity, or any of the warm-up or energizers activities on pp. 92–9 and 113–117.

Comfort breaks

Time – 5 to 10 minutes, depending on location.

Purpose – to visit the loo or as a light energy break.

Comment – only useful as an energy break if physical, not mental, energy is flagging. If the former, then use an energizer as a brain and spirit refresher, too.

Review breaks

Time – 5 to 30 minutes or longer.

Purpose – to raise energy and reinforce learning.

Comment – either schedule in or use short review activities (see pp. 106–112) ad hoc to revise points of learning and practise skills while also refreshing the energy in the room.

Jot down any thoughts you have for your own session.

BLUFFER'S GUIDE TO FACILITATION

Confidence in yourself

First, and most importantly, have confidence in yourself: your ability to facilitate, your faith in the outcome of the session, your design of the session. The last two should be no problem if you apply the methods in this book; the first can be helped by examining and, if necessary, changing your beliefs about yourself and your participants (see pp. 5–10), and then will build rapidly as you lead successful workshops.

Quick fix

Take two minutes to close your eyes and imagine the end of a phenomenally successful session that you have just led. Really get into it: how you're feeling, what your participants are saying to you and each other, their pleased expressions, the great evaluation forms. Take as long as you need to create a totally whole-body experience of having achieved a great result and being proud of it. Now, make an association between that feeling and a gesture of some kind (squeezing two fingers together, clenching your fist, etc.) and either use this gesture to recall the feeling or repeat the process of closing your eyes and having the cinematographic experience of being there. Each time you do this you build a neural pathway in your brain towards a successful outcome, so on the day in a sense the brain already knows how to 'get' there. In addition, it's a great way of preventing nerves, since worry is simply doing the opposite: imagining the worst possible outcome.

Rapport with the group

What does that mean? To me, it means feeling at home with the group, getting a high level of participation from them during whole-group discussions, warm responses from them when you drop in on their pairs or small group work to coach or check in and willingness to join in with all exercises, however unusual (for example BrainGym). But you can start this process even before you meet them by using prework – create the right impression and you're halfway towards creating positive expectations of the workshop and assumptions about you. If it's your team you're facilitating, there's nothing to stop you still sending out prework that's so different from previous communications from you that their assumptions about the workshop session at the very least might be confounded.

Quick fix

As part of the prework, get your participants to complete a fun puzzle related to the subject in some way for a small prize on arrival. Where possible, also get them to return their expectations and wishes for the workshop, whatever the subject – even if it's just mandatory training. Every bit helps you to build personal gains into your design – even if it's a briefing on the latest health and safety policy, if you know what they're expecting from it, you're either forewarned or tipped off as to ways to guarantee that at least some will get what they came for. When they arrive, try to speak to everyone personally before you get started so you and they have built some familiarity – and this applies even if it's your team, as it's a chance for you to play to a different side of you. During the day, whenever possible, work with the pairs and small groups in a coaching capacity – this is, of course, made very easy when you have designed a highly participative day and one of the many benefits of interactivity.

Good design will do most of the work for you

This is really true! As I hope you can see from this book so far, the more engaged, bought-in and focused your participants are, the easier it is to for them to have a really positive experience, learn loads, apply it easily and take away good memories of what possibly could even have been a boring topic. There are so many ways for you to do this that even applying only a quarter of what's set out in this book will pay immense dividends.

Quick fix

Any ideas from this book! As the barest minimum, if you do nothing else use RSVP (see p. 42) – i.e., ensure your session involves reasoning, sound, vision and physical movement.

Ask intelligent questions

By 'intelligent' I mean ones that stimulate your participants' intellect and get them to reply using more than 'Yes' or 'No' – commonly called 'open' questions. In addition, encourage participants to focus on what worked after each exercise and, in particular, which bits can they apply back in the 'real world'. Everyone finds criticism easy, so focusing on the positive of a new experience or skill is the harder option – this is where intelligent questions really help.

Quick fix

These are the kinds of questions to keep around you and use liberally.

- 'How could you . . .?'
- 'What did you . . .?'
- 'Where will you . . .?'
- 'When will you . . .?'
- 'What worked for you?'
- 'How could you apply that to . . .?'
- 'How did that go?'
- 'Who else needs to be involved?'
- To deal with 'Yes, but's, ask, 'So, how could you apply this *even though* [insert subject of yes, but]?' or 'So how could you apply this *and* [insert *opposite* of subject of yes, but]?'

Don't be an 'expert'

Try to avoid the temptation of appearing an 'expert' in the subject – even if you are. Not only can this set you up on a pedestal from which you could fall spectacularly, but it's also far easier to allow the group to discover for themselves – with your skilful facilitation and guidance – the wonders of the subject and how to apply it. Another pitfall of being the expert is a propensity to share your experience with those new to the area, the problem being that it is *your* experience and theirs may well turn out to be different. Answer questions, by all means, illuminate stuck areas and guide them out of obviously wrong turns, but endeavour to keep the focus on *their* discovery and allow them their *own* experience of the subject you're sharing unless specifically asked for yours.

Quick fix

Keeping the design oriented towards participant-centred activities is an easy way of doing this. You can then go among them as a coach while they're working, picking up any common misunderstandings for the debrief afterwards and using the debriefs as a 'mop-up' to the main learning of the exercises. In this way, ironically, you will probably appear more expert than if you'd tried by staying up front and sharing all your knowledge, as the discussions will be focused on what is most meaningful to them: their recent experiences with the material and its application.

Focus on process, not content

This is a great skill to develop, as it's very easy – in fact, the norm – to get sucked into the content of discussions, exercises, etc., and get so carried away with trying to solve an individual problem that, before you know it, 20 minutes have passed and, while one individual is getting their issue solved, the rest of the group members are decidedly bored or worse. Try to keep one eye always on the time and the focus of the teams, group, pairs or individuals on the outcome of each exercise. Most of all, keep your own outcomes for the session and each section/exercise clearly in mind so that you can tell instantly if it's slipping out of sight.

Quick fix

Make it a discipline to read your own outcomes before explaining each section/exercise and ensure you have stated the outcome of the exercise clearly each time. This will help the group members to 'police' each other and stay on track. If the main purpose of the exercise is to practise skills (albeit on a real issue), then don't be afraid to pull people in and remind them of that focus to prevent them wading into the content. The sooner they get the skills under their belt, the faster they'll solve *all* such issues.

Keep your group busy, focused, outcome-led and bought-in

As I've reiterated throughout this book, the busier you can keep your group members:

- the happier they'll be;
- the more they'll learn;
- the more likely they'll be to use the skills or knowledge; and
- the better their (and your) experience of the workshop.

Quick fix

Again, use the tips from this book, particularly:

- exercise suggestions/RSVP (to keep them busy and active, though remember the need for downtime) – see pp. 92–117;
- outcome setting (to keep focused) – see pp. 11–14;
- linguistic tips (for buy-in) – see pp. 118–128.

3

CHAPTER THREE
Building a great session

This section has a timeline and three main parts.

Timeline – a three-month countdown to the execution of a workshop and beyond (strictly optional; see Figure 3.1).

1 Strong framework – what goes where

- Structure and flow

- Theming

- The title

- The Welcome Pack

2 Step-by-step activities – how exactly you'll achieve your outcomes

- Metaphors and their use

- Introduction and welcome

- BrainGym

- Off-the-shelf activities (various types)

- Tricks of the trade

- Strong finish

- Evaluation

- Setting the scene on the day – room preparation to complement your design

- Follow-through

3 Materials – last because now you know what you need

- Canny material design

- Participants' materials

- Your materials

Figure 3.1 Time checklist

Time frame	Public workshop[1]	Private workshop[2]	Notes
T = 3 months	Know what your subject is and its main benefits First adverts out – flyers, posters in local windows, e-mail or e-newsletter announcements, newsgroups/lists, local or national radio if interesting subject, direct mail, other orgs or businesses whose customers are your target audience See 'Cunning linguistics', p. 120, for copywriting and linguistic tips Venue sought and ideally booked; check cancellation policy before agreeing anything Sort out/delegate the logistics of accommodation (if applicable), dietary needs (a question for the joining instructions/Welcome Pack), accessibility of venue	Know what your subject is and its main benefits If likely to be repeat work or large roll-out, agree a pilot workshop with client if at all possible See 'Cunning linguistics', p. 120, for tips on writing copy and linguistics Sort out/delegate the logistics of accommodation (if applicable), dietary needs (a question for the joining instructions/Welcome Pack), accessibility of venue	For both running workshops and meeting and selling to clients, NLP skills are immensely useful – sign up to an introduction to NLP or Practitioner course if you don't already have these skills Pilot workshops – whether for public or private use – are a great way of trying out new ideas or exercises. If you can arrange one, do it
T = 2 months	Start design (content, main structure and headings); enough to alert you to any research you need to do before detailed design Do any research necessary (Google is an invaluable resource) Second or third round of promotional activity	Start design (content, main structure and headings); enough to alert you to any research you need to do before detailed design Do any research necessary (Google is an invaluable resource) Meet with stakeholder/client(s) and agree top-level design plus contact person for admin/venue arrangements Ensure roles are clear (i.e. who sends out materials/prework/	When marketing a workshop, consider mutually beneficial partnerships with other businesses or organizations that already have a good database of your customers. This can be a creative way of reaching more people for less cost in time and money

Figure 3.1 continued

Time frame	Public workshop[1]	Private workshop[2]	Notes
		joining instructions, who chases up participants, who liaises with venue, etc.)	
T = 1 month	Next level of design (structure, subheads, ideas for exercises, some ideas for materials) if you're a Type 2, or detailed design if you're a Type 1[3] Early-bird discounts should be over and most people signed up ready for any prework to be sent out Caterers informed of final numbers, venue contact informed of room layout and equipment requirements	Stakeholders involved in design for sign-off purposes – get them to sign and approve the outcomes for the whole session and each section; this way they agree the *what*, leaving you free to choose the *how*. Include proposed materials, prework ideas, follow-up and management buy-in/support post-workshop Get numbers finalized if possible View venue you'll be in if possible to give you a 'feel' for room layout – at the very least find out the size and flexibility of layout arrangements Agree min/max numbers with stakeholders if possible to avoid either overcrowding or too-small groups (though I once did run a successful workshop with only 3 participants, I don't recommend it) Go/no go decision may need to be made depending on cancellation arrangements if external venue	Early-bird discounts are worth doing as they help you get people signed up within the time frame allowed by most cancellation policies on external venues When finding a venue, look for newly created rooms that need the business, out-of-the-ordinary places like country park visitor centres, etc. and do whatever you can to build a good relationship with them if you like the location
T = 3 weeks	Go/no go decision depending on numbers and venue cancellation policy	Get sign-off for all proposed materials and follow-up	
T = 2 weeks	Detailed design if you're a Type 2 (though even this might be a bit early, depending on other commitments) All prework sent out Go/no go decision should be made	Go/no go decision should be made on numbers if within organization (some will leave it later)	
T = 1 week	Detailed design if you're a very busy Type 2, plus prework sent out at the last minute (no later than a week before to allow participants the time to do it) Materials printed and ready if Type 1, designed and in production if Type 2	Detailed design All prework sent out As for public	

Figure 3.1 continued

Time frame	Public workshop[1]	Private workshop[2]	Notes
T = 2 days	Finalize all venue arrangements and call any participants you're unsure of (in terms of attendance) Any last-minute purchases made (e.g. chocs for prizes) Write up any pre-prepared flipcharts (enlist the help of any artistic friends and family if your drawings are as bad as mine)	Double-double-check venue arrangements, group numbers and start/finish with your client, boss, stakeholder and/or contact person in case any last-minute changes haven't filtered down to you As for public	Make sure any printing is done; leaving it to the day before leaves you wide open to printer or photocopier failure and any other of a range of last-minute glitches
T = day before	Do whatever works best for you to ensure a good night's sleep and a great state of mind	As for public	With luck, you're chilled and ready
T = session day	Ensure you're on site at least an hour before arrival time – more if room set-up is complicated, or even night before (e.g. themed) to sort out or check room layout, write up any last-minute flips you've thought of, make it 'home', etc.	As for public	The earlier you're there, the more time you have to get 'settled in' and gain a sense of familiarity with your surroundings that will add to your confidence when meeting the group
T = end of session	Thank relevant staff and leave room as tidy as you can to minimize their work; I leave any excess chocs for them to sweeten the job Try not to analyse how well it went or even to read the feedback forms (if you're using them) until tomorrow Take with you all written-on flipcharts for ideas to feed into later versions of this workshop and disposal	Leave room as tidy as you can, thank contact person and staff As for public	Though it may not be 'your job' to tidy the room other than removing your materials, and though you might be tired, some quick basic tidying is usually appreciated by the organizers and will help build a good relationship with the venue staff
T = day after	After a good night's sleep, now's the time to decide how well it went and, while it's fresh in your mind, what you'd do differently next time Capture any thoughts you have about re-jigging the design even if you're not willing to go into detail just yet, as they fade very quickly	Contact boss/stakeholder or client for feedback both sides As for public	If you can bear it, now is a good time to write up any changes to your training notes that you'd make if you ran it again – at the very least make sure your scribbles are legible and capture all your current thoughts for later translation

Figure 3.1 continued

Time frame	Public workshop[1]	Private workshop[2]	Notes
T = 2–3 weeks after	Usual time for follow-up coaching, check-in call or any other follow-through agreed with group	As for public	Well done!

Notes:

[1] Offered to general public, involving hire of premises, advertising, etc.

[2] Offered inhouse, already contracted to do, as employee/consultant – I'm assuming it's already sold-in and agreed.

[3] There are two main types of designers (according to the well-respected and probably valid research of Highmore Sims, 2006): Type 1, who approach it methodically and like to have every-thing buttoned down well in advance of the session date in case of changes or emergencies . . . or 'just in case'. Type 2 designers, on the other hand, are happy to deal with the top-level design of headings and vagueish benefits and will leave anything remotely detailed to the last possible minute, then do the detailed design in a flurry of stressed 'creativity'. This manual will help both types. I'm not saying which I am.

Strong framework

STRUCTURE AND FLOW

Ideally, your sections will follow a sequence that makes logical sense. For example, Figure 3.2 gives the top-level subject headings in a logical order if I were going to run a workshop based on this book.

Looking at what you have, take a few moments to run through the following questions and think about your own session.

- What are the main sections (and subsections)? Try to stick to four if possible for a one-day workshop.

- Do your sections group naturally in any way? If so, where are the best places for these sections in terms of section size – before/after lunch? Before/after break?

- What about subsections? How can you link each section/subsection in a way that makes sense and builds on the anticipation you created with your pre-session contact or marketing?

- If there's no clear connection between them, how can you present the headings in such a way that an impression of continuity is given?

- What common threads can you draw out or what context can you put around them that will bring them together into more of a 'package'?

- Where are the obvious 'ebbs and flows' in terms of energy? For example, do some sections have more theory or are going to be necessarily less interactive than others? Energetically, 'brainwork' is best done in the morning where possible.

- What subtle or more obvious threads run through sections that can be used as links with visuals, musical breaks/background, colours, possible themes, even objects to reinforce the learning and flow?

Figure 3.2 Day template

AM 1	AM 2	B R E A K	AM 3	AM 4
Intro	**Beliefs** *Best place for 'thinking sections' is before lunch*		**Design logistics**	**Whole-brain learning** *High-energy section just before lunch when energy flagging*
LUNCH				
PM 1	PM 2	B R E A K	PM 3	PM 4
Whole-brain learning *High-energy session continued after lunch to prevent post-prandial drowsiness*	**Building session** *Application of theory to 'live' work*		**Building session** *Continued*	**Materials Next steps** *Taking the learning out to their own projects*

- Each segment is approximately 45 mins.
- Morning formal break held approximately 1½ hrs after start, for 15 to 20 mins.
- Lunch minimum of 45 mins.
- For balance, have morning slightly longer than afternoon when there is a choice.

Timings

The next step is to put times around your subsections. If you're using the day template, time chunks are already built in, but they're not cast in stone and you might want to change them for various reasons:

- you want to pay a lot of attention to one particular aspect of your subject;

- there's limited time to cover a lot of material so you feel you can't afford to take a break;

- a particular exercise you have in mind will not fit into a 45-minute time slot, but you think it's perfect for the subject.

So long as you stay attentive to your group's energy levels, it's acceptable to go for longer than the suggested 45 minutes before a break; in fact, it's generally pretty common, but often for the wrong reasons.

So now what you should have is your:

- main headings;

- subsections within those headings;

- rough order of sections and subsections;

- an idea of time for each subsection (made easy if you use the template, but ideally 40–45 minutes).

Learning outcomes

These, though often considered a bit of a chore to do when designing a session, can make your job a lot easier at the end when it comes to evaluation.

- When designing a workshop for a boss or client, having clear, *agreed* outcomes makes the job easier to design and far easier to measure at the end.

- When working with the public, getting sign-up to your session on the basis of well-written learning outcomes practically guarantees met expectations – provided you then deliver to them, of course!

- Writing detailed learning outcomes for a section can suggest the exercise(s) to go into it, saving design time . . . having said that, it's often easier to do them at the end, when you know what you've designed.

- Setting learning outcomes for each section is a good way of further sorting the wheat from the chaff when deciding what to include and discard – if you can't turn the material into a learning outcome, it is probably either information only or irrelevant content.

So how do you do it?

Writing learning outcomes

There is a standard, and pretty useful, formula and, when I'm using learning outcomes (not always, it has to be said), it's what I apply:

'By the end of this [session/section/exercise], participants will be able to [action verb] in [context]'

Let's break it down (bear with me).

'*By the end of this [session, etc.]*' – it doesn't matter what they're doing during the session, so long as they can do X by the end of it. This is important when it comes to getting sign-off from clients, sign-up from the public, etc. as it gives you the flexibility to deliver the *how* however you like, so long as they get the *what*.

'*participants will be able to . . .*' – this means that they will be able to, in theory at least, show what they have learned if required. If you use 'participants will know . . .' that's far harder to evaluate unless you're going to use an exam to prove it. Using 'be able to . . .' encourages you to convert that into a measurable action.

'. . . *[action verb]* . . .' – this ensures that you attach a real output from the learning input in the form of something they can now *do* differently, whether that be listing the seven signs of ageing (better than '*knowing* the seven signs' because it's testing it by definition), sawing a woman in half, etc.

'. . . *in [context]*' – this part adds depth and specificity and is often left out. It should include the 'with whom, when, where, with what'. For example, 'saw a woman in half' is a fairly dubious skill until you attach '. . . using a magician's box in five minutes with an assistant'. Equally, 'list the seven signs of ageing' isn't very specific if you're a vet without '. . . identifiable through cage bars in dormice when hibernating'. It tells the participants what they're signing up to, what they can expect, and how and where it will be useful. And it reminds you to include the application.

List of 'action words' suitable for learning outcomes

Agree	Exercise
Analyse	Explain
Apply	Explore
Carry out	Generate
Change	Identify
Choose	Introduce
Commit	List
Create	Pace
Demonstrate	Practise/practice
Describe	Present
Design	Produce
Detail	Recognize
Develop	Risk assess
Discuss	Share
Elicit	Transform
Establish	Turn
Evaluate	Use

The key for a valid learning outcome word is can it be observed and/or measured in some way?

And so now it's your turn. Use the form overleaf to run through your session, writing learning outcomes for each main section. I would suggest that for a day's workshop you have one overall learning outcome for the day, then between four and eight section outcomes. By 'sections' I mean those between main breaks.

Exercise

Learning outcomes worksheet

(**Top tip:** come back and do these again at the very end, when you've designed the whole workshop – it makes it a lot easier!)

'**By the end of this** [section], **you will be able to** [action verb] **in/when/with/out** [context]'

Session title: _____

Overall session outcome:

Learning outcomes

Section 1:

Section 2:

Section 3:

Section 4:

Section 5:

Section 6:

Section 7:

Section 8:

Features and benefits

Looking at both your public and learning outcomes, we're now going to translate them into 'sexier' language that you can use to help entice your audience through the door.

First, nip down the following table, writing each specific skill or nugget of knowledge your group will have at the end of their time with you.

Then for each what that will mean to them in the 'real world'. At this point we just need an overview of each section or topic you'll be covering, with no need for detail within it in terms of subsections or exercises.

A tip: for each one-day workshop, try to think in numbers divisible by 4, e.g. four or eight main headings for a day workshop; two or four for a half day; one or two for a taster, etc. This is helpful when you come to divide the session into chunks of time for the detailed design.

Skill/knowledge you're planning to impart	What they'll be able to do, know, avoid or stop as a result of using said skill/knowledge in the real world
e.g. awareness of body language	*e.g. be able to identify and respond to non-verbal signals; prevent needless misunderstandings; get on people's wavelength faster; become more 'intuitive'*

Less is more

At this point I'd like you to take a brief step back, look once more at your content and ask yourself this question: do I have too much?

It's common for first-timers (or fourth- or even 200th-timers) to put too much material into a session in the fear that they will otherwise run out of things to do and the group will sit staring at them in demanding silence or that there won't be enough to provide 'value'.

In my experience, this never happens. What happens far more often is the 'Oh-hell-we'll-never-have-time-for-that-I'd-better-rush-them-through-this-bit-then-decide-which-bit-to-drop-after-break' situation.

Less is most definitely *more* when it comes to learning. It's far better to get across one concept thoroughly and well – by which I mean comprehension, relevant applications and, if applicable, practice – than gallop through several topics briefly on a heap of slides, leaving the participants to sort out the application themselves sometime after the workshop . . . which of course often means sometime never.

The other thing to consider is that if you are moving to a more facilitative style, each section will take far longer than a presentation would. It's much quicker to tell an audience something than have them work it out for themselves or convey it interactively; more than twice as long in some cases.

So quickly revisit your plan and see if you can prune anything out at all. It may be that the pruning will take place later, but it's worth having a quick look now in order to save potential wasted time working up something you'll discard later.

THEMING

Sometimes it's appropriate – and not only appropriate but advisable – to theme your workshop (or series).

By 'theme' I don't mean the topic, as in 'The theme for today is Communication'. I mean *theming*, as in using a pirate theme or a James Bond theme. Fancy dress for learning, if you will.

Theming can confer the following benefits (and probably a host more).

- Remove negative 'classroom' associations that many adults still have with anything remotely linked to learning.

- Create interest – both before and during the session(s).

- Improve recall – theming makes the session different from most 'chalk and talk' training room events and therefore more memorable.

- Aid learning – a well-chosen theme can add greatly to the learning both in terms of the learning experience and also what is implicitly conveyed (see Appendix 1 for more details on this).

- Make the session more enjoyable, both for the participants and the facilitator – this in turn aids recall, since long-term memory is situated next to emotions in the brain.

- It can act as a powerful metaphor that stays in the mind and reinforces the learning long after the actual event and exercises are forgotten. This, to me, is the best use for themes and should *always* be considered when deciding to use one (see 'Metaphors and their use' for full exploration of this subject, pp. 83–7).

The potential downsides to theming are as follows.

- It can involve a lot more work in terms of set-up, particularly if you're going to do a full-scale theme with room visuals, themed exercises, prework, accessories, etc.

- If not done convincingly – by which I mean *you're* not convinced by it – it can fall flat and even get in the way of learning. However, never be put off by naysayers claiming that your group 'won't go for it' or the like. Any group will be carried along by a convinced – and therefore convincing – facilitator. All you have to do is be sure of it yourself.

So, if you're tempted by the idea, how do you go about choosing a good theme?

The questions below should help get you started, and see also Appendix 1 where there's a table of a few of my favourites for you to peruse, together with suggestions of where you might use each theme and what might be conveyed implicitly by the inherent metaphor.

Finding the right theme for your session

- Is there an obvious analogy or metaphor that explains your subject, or aspects of it? What is your subject like *(e.g. communication is like a dance, time management is like juggling . . .)*?

- What additional, perhaps even implicit, skills or mindset do you want your participants to take away with them, and how could a theme help that *(e.g. resourceful and determined as a hero or stimulated and creative as DaVinci)*?

- How do you want your participants to feel as they leave the room at the end of the session and how could a theme encourage that *(e.g. relaxed and in a holiday mood, excited about new possibilities)*?

- What hobbies, interests, passions, addictions (care with this one!) do you have that you could incorporate? *(I once used a* Changing Rooms *theme very effectively, allowing me to indulge my addiction to house-transformation programmes as well as apply an effective learning tool.)*

THE TITLE

It wouldn't be fair when covering 'packaging' of your session or series of sessions to leave out the all-important title. Generally I don't settle on a final title for each programme or session until I've got my framework and possibly theme bolted down, which is why it's here.

So what are you going to call your session, programme, seminar, workshop? Naming is very important in terms of what associations you could create in the minds of your audience.

Will you go for a 'Ronseal' approach and name it according to what it will do for your participants? What about an abstract name that will evoke certain images or emotions? How about a play on words?

My e-book, *The Magical Business Name Machine,* offers a complete, simple but foolproof process for generating creative yet relevant names for services, products or businesses; but, for a toe-in-the-water approach, you could try the answering the following on the accompanying mindmap.

> **Benefits branch:** Think about what people will gain from attending (and this applies equally to an inhouse briefing or meeting as to an external or public programme). How will this time spent with you benefit them, personally and professionally?

> **Values branch:** What's important to you about the session or the subject it covers? Why are you running it anyway? If you're a manager and it's because you have to, what would you personally like to get out of the experience?

> **Experience branch:** Finally, what do you want them to think, feel or say about the session in weeks, months or even years to come when they look back on it? Even if it's a 'dry', routine subject you're having to brief them on, what memory would you *like* them to have?

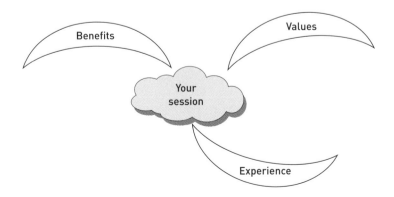

THE WELCOME PACK

As outlined earlier in this book, the Welcome Pack is a great way of preparing your participants for the upcoming session, warming them up and getting them to think about what they want from it.

It's generally best to put it together after you've created the framework and theme for your session at least – though, if your schedule permits, creating it alongside the other participants' materials helps to give it the same 'look'.

More than just 'joining instructions', it should set the tone for your session – be personal, friendly, convey something of your personality. It is acting as an ambassador for you and the session, as it will be the first 'official' contact your participants have had from you in relation to this session.

This is just as important whether you're about to meet a new group or are running a session for your own team: it's a chance to shape or reshape expectations, start the process off and start getting results before they even walk into the room.

Even if your admin team always send out the 'joining instructions', make sure you have an input into the design – it's your impression they're creating.

So, as a minimum, a Welcome Pack should include:

● a personal welcome or letter from you;

● some kind of exercise, task or question to get them thinking about the subject before the day – keep this relatively light unless you have good reason or have given them advance warning (no more than an hour's work);

● an outline of the session/process – top level only, to allow you greatest time flexibility;

● any time commitments related to follow-on or project groups they need to be aware of up front;

● a map and directions where applicable.

Tips to make it appealing:

- use RSVP (see p. 42) – the more senses involved, the better.

- don't be afraid of a light tone and personal touch – whether 'professional' or not, they're still human beings.

- keep text light and use graphics wherever possible.

Following is an example of a Welcome Pack I sent out recently for my career change programme. Feel free to copy the format.

Meanwhile, have a think about what you could include yourself.

Your Welcome Pack

Personal letter – what would make it typically 'you'? What needs to go in it in terms of information? What about something about yourself? Do they need to bring anything with them on the day?

Task/exercise – what could you get them doing before the day that will easily feed into one of the first activities? How could you get them interacting with each other? What elements play more to the intrapersonal intelligence and are therefore better suited to being done alone?

Outline of session and/or process – how could you make the outline look visually interesting? Is it themed? Can you use graphics related to the theme?

Time commitments – when and how long is the session? Are there any related commitments, such as project groups, coaching sessions, follow-up calls that they need to have in their diaries?

Map/directions – how could you make these more interesting? Could you link them with the theme (e.g. for a pirate theme you could print the map out on parchment and use ancient font for the directions)?

Example Welcome Pack

[INSERT LOGO/NAME ETC.]

9 October 2005

Dear

Thank you for registering for 'In-Vocation'. This is Stage 1 of the programme and in this pack you will find the following.

- A four-part self-study exercise: this is quite detailed. Please set aside time to do it properly (an hour or two), as the more time you can give it, the more you will get from it. Please bring the completed sheets to the workshop, as you will be using them there for one of the exercises.

- A full outline of the workshop day.

- An appointment for your coaching session.

- Instructions on how to get to . . . .

I've always believed that people should do what they love and love what they do and, personally, I have changed my career radically several times in order to maintain that fresh motivation. Along the way I've helped many others do the same in my capacity as a trainer, coach and writer and I really look forward to meeting you on this part of your particular journey.

I hope you enjoy the exercise, and, if you have any queries about it please feel free to call me. If I am not in, leave a message and I will get back to you as soon as I can.

Have fun!

With warm regards,

Nikki Highmore Sims

▶

Who do you do?

Who do you do?

This is to help you uncover the key **role** lurking behind your urge to change direction . . .

THE PROCESS

1 Around the mindmaps below, or on small sticky notes, write as many *positive* roles (and feel free to make terms up, e.g. 'encourager', 'energy-generator', rather than only using 'proper' roles such as 'teacher') as you feel you ever fulfil now or have done in the past (and enjoyed it!).

2 First, do this for 'Work', then 'Personal'.

3 Now compare the two categories. Are there any common themes emerging?

4 Play around with different combinations of terms and roles until you find one (or more) that fits you in some way *every day*, no matter what you may be doing – the important part is that it definitely applies some way each day.

5 Feel free to involve family, friends and colleagues – don't be restricted to what goes on in your own head! Sometimes another person can point out something that's blindingly obvious to them (and others, but you're too close to see it.

6 Take as much time as you need to get something that reflects the essential you at your deepest level and that you are very happy with.

7 Once you've found one or more combinations that really fit, write your ROLE(s) in the box.

▶

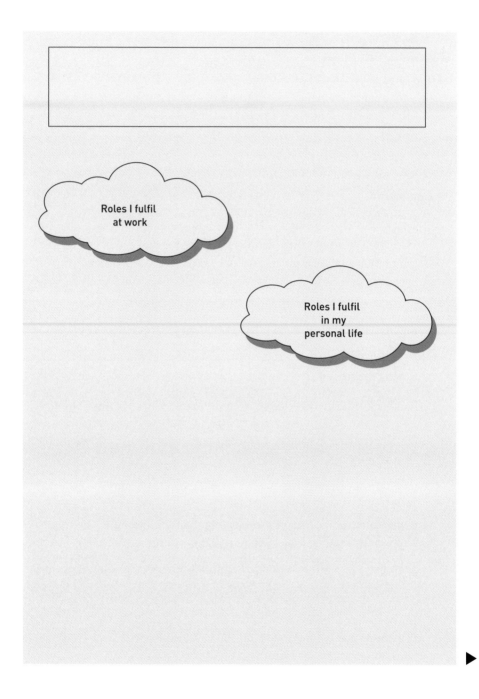

Workshop outline

Timings: 10am to 5pm; arrive at 9.45 for registration/coffee. There will be a morning and afternoon break.

AM: EXPLORATION AND INSPIRATION

- RAVE-ing start
- What gives you energy?
- What hints has your life been giving you?
- Guided journey
- Create-a-character
- Global to local

Lunch

PM: TURNING AN IDEA INTO REALITY

- Idea generator
- Outcome setting
- Disney strategy
- Next steps
- Awards ceremony

NB: Individual exercises may differ slightly on the day, but the overall structure and aims of the workshop will remain the same.

▶

Follow-up coaching session

Your appointment is:* _____

This is a 30-minute telephone coaching session. Please call 0845 6442344 (or 01905 764117 if you have a telephone provider that offers free calls to anything other than non-geographical numbers) at the appointed time, and we will spend the time working on any issues that have arisen since the workshop and accelerating the next steps you want to take.

If this time and/or date is inconvenient, we can arrange a mutually suitable time at the workshop – please bring your diary.

Step-by-step activities

Now you have the overview and structure of your session, it's time to put some meat on the bones. This section will take you through a variety of activities, tools and approaches that you can feed into the different parts of your workshop/session, starting with the introduction and ending (unsurprisingly) with the finish.

Setting up the room is considered after the finish and I go into some considerable detail. Though on one level it may seem odd to have the room set-up last in the sequence, you would generally consider it only after you know exactly what activities and themes the room will need to support.

METAPHORS AND THEIR USE

This is actually a natural bed-partner to theming – and, indeed, one of the most valuable reasons for using it.

This immensely handy device is one of the power tools in your workshop design toolkit. It's a highly expedient way of reaching both conscious and subconscious learning states instantaneously, plus sending a deep seed into the memory to boot.

So I'm into metaphors, but how exactly can they be applied? Well, in the previous paragraph I used the metaphor of a power tool to describe metaphors and the metaphor of a toolkit to describe the skill set used when designing a workshop.

By describing a new or complex concept by drawing a parallel with a day-to-day activity, object or action, you formulate a clear image in the mind, allow the imagination to 'try it on' and speak a simpler language to that of the conceptual part of the brain. A simple question to ask yourself when generating metaphors is 'What is it like?'[2]

---

[2] Before the pedants of the world rise up against me, yes, I'm fully aware of the literary distinction between a metaphor and a simile. However, for the purposes of illustrating learning (unless your subject is literature!), similes and metaphors are lumped together functionally as one unit.

Here are some more.

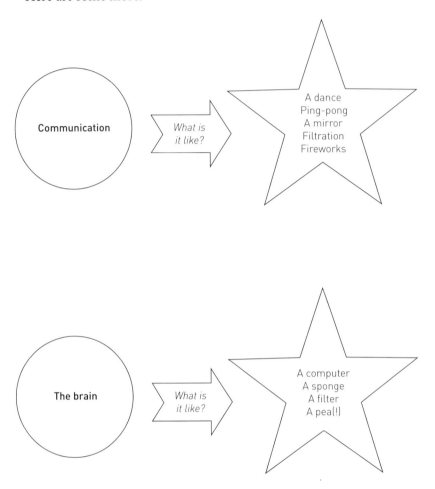

Exercise

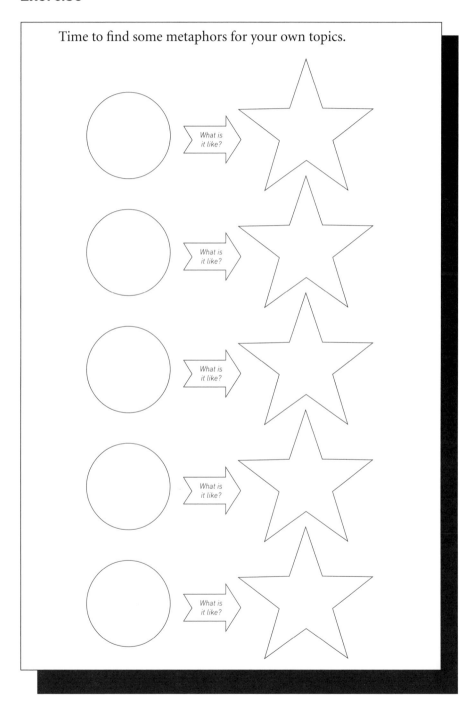

Time to find some metaphors for your own topics.

What makes a good metaphor?

Not all metaphors are good ones – some should most definitely be left in the minds that created them. How do you tell the difference?

This quick checklist might help.

- Can others see a clear and obvious link between your concept and the metaphor you're using to put it across? If you have to explain it or it seems 'forced', it's failed this test.

- Does it have any negative connotations? 'Battle' is a very popular metaphor to describe communication (just read the newspapers and notice the way they describe parliamentary debate) and illness, for example. However, there is always a loser in battle, plus casualties. Make sure your metaphor has no implied negativity.

- If your metaphor is to be used in the design of the session or any element of it, including materials, is there enough flexibility in it to accommodate all the aspects of your topic? For example, 'sponge' works as a metaphor for the brain when considering its appearance and how it soaks up everything around it, but it comes up short compared with the 'computer' metaphor when it comes to explaining areas of function.

If your metaphor is obvious, positive and flexible, you have a good one. Go forth and utilize it!

Using metaphors

So now you've generated lots of imaginative metaphors, what can you use them for? Here are a few of the ways you can sew them into the fabric of your session.

- As explanations to aid the understanding of an abstract or simply new concept, mechanism, etc. You can use them in this way verbally or in your visual aids and/or design of the room (along with theming where appropriate).

- An alternative and more interesting way of saying something (such as 'sew them into the fabric of your session' versus 'use them').

- It conveys the 'why' more effectively than bald explanation alone – how much easier is it to understand the importance of 'good-quality' thoughts when one realizes that the unconscious mind operates like a computer and acts on everything we 'tell' it?

- A memorable way of using association and the right brain to retain information. For example, image consultants hit upon using the seasons to group the colours they use with their clients: memorable and marketable.

- This brings me to marketing. Having an effective metaphor makes marketing easier as it provides a creative 'hook' for the framework and materials, ideas for branding, even target markets.

How can you start to use metaphors in your session?

INTRODUCTION AND WELCOME

Now you have a structure for your session and know roughly what's going to be covered and where, you can start to think about exactly how you're going to get it all across.

So you've got them in the room, will have sent out a Welcome Pack that's helped to get them in the mood (to be designed after you thoroughly know what you're going to do and how) and prepared the most fabulous environment for them.

What next?

It's time to welcome them properly. Be yourself, meet 'n' greet, help them feel as at home in the room as you will be yourself.

Meeting and greeting

Here are some suggestions for things to cover before you plunge into your first exercise (and forgive me where/if I state the obvious).

- Meet them proactively as they come in – don't leave them wondering if you're the facilitator.

- Chat informally with as many as you can to establish familiarity, find out about them, perhaps find out what they're most looking forward to (if in-house or public workshop) and/or had attracted them to the session (if a public workshop).

- Have refreshments ready and waiting from about 30 minutes before official start time.

- Change music or volume when ready to start.

- Start on time unless you have a good reason not to (e.g. a message from one participant saying they'll be ten minutes late or only half the participants there).

- Open by 'pacing and leading' – that is, state some obvious facts first (for example, where they've come from, the weather, something about the location/room) so they've established mental agreement with you, then introduce some of the benefits of the session (particularly important if you suspect or know they don't really want to be there).

- Give a *very* brief (i.e. two minutes or shorter) introduction of who you are, then get straight into the warm-up exercise (make it relevant to the day's topic). (See pp. 92–6 for warm-up exercise ideas.)

- Debrief the warm-up, during which time you could have people talk about themselves and their experiences (if you've sat people in small groups and used a team warm-up exercise, this is made doubly easier as the participants will already have built a degree of familiarity with each other and will feel more comfortable speaking in the large group than if starting from 'cold').

- Fuller intro. Now you all know each other better, and they're warmed up and ready to get going, they'll be more likely to listen attentively as you explain more fully who you are and why you're leading this session and what's in store for them. Mention the usual professional points of confidentiality, punctuality and mobile phone silence! Also where the toilets and fire exits are and roughly how many breaks they'll have.

- I recommend you don't attribute times to each activity when giving the overview and, in fact, even try to avoid stating what's before and after lunch unless you've run the session a dozen times and definitely know the timings. This gives you maximum flexibility in the event of shorter- or longer-than-planned exercises and frees the group from being distracted by process changes.

- For the session's outline, first show the overview (on a brown paper wall timeline or colourful list of the session's main topics) and then what each section will entail, with the emphasis on benefits (but see 'Cunning linguistics', pp. 118–28, for language tips).

- At this point you might want to introduce some of your support materials.

- Finally (for the introduction), it's time to introduce the first main exercise – and if you want a really great way to do that, use the 4mat . . .

The 4mat

Have you ever wanted a nifty way of introducing a presentation or exercise that gets your audience's attention right from the start? Well, I'm about to share with you a simple linguistic tool that does just that. It gives you a compelling introduction any time you want it. It's a simple formula that you can learn in minutes and apply endlessly. Also, it's not just for facilitation: you can use this tool any time you need to 'sell' something, whether in front of a client, in a boardroom or even at interview.

That was an example of it: the '4mat'. Based on a teaching tool devised by Bernice McCarthy, the 4mat has been adapted for use as a linguistic tool by communication trainers and experts and it's such a versatile and simple tool that I want to share it with you for use in your sessions and indeed just about anywhere else.

Think of something in your workshop you'd like a strong introduction for – it could even be the whole session – and then work through the following four stages with it.

1 The why

Open with a question that gets the person/audience searching inside themselves for a similar experience or any question that will have them wanting to know more.

My e.g.: 'Have you ever wanted a nifty way of introducing a presentation . . .?'

Your e.g.:

2 The what

Tell them what it is that they'll be learning/buying/hearing about, with a focus on its benefits.

My e.g.: 'Well, I'm about to share with you a simple linguistic tool that does just that. It gives you a compelling introduction any time you need one.'

Your e.g.:

3 The how

Next, outline the process: how the 'what' will come about.

My e.g.: 'It's a simple formula that you can learn in minutes and apply endlessly.'

Your e.g.:

4 What else

Finally, close on how or where else your audience will be able to use/apply what you're sharing with them or any additional benefits.

My e.g.: 'Also, it's not just for facilitation: you can use this tool any time you need to 'sell' something, whether in front of a client, in a boardroom or even at interview.'

Your e.g.:

Warm-up v. 'ground rules'

In my personal and professional career I've attended dozens, possibly scores, of personal and professional development workshops and training programmes and I confess I have never yet seen the point or benefit of a very 'trainery' thing: 'contracting' or setting 'ground rules'.

In case you haven't come across this, it's an exercise, usually taking around half an hour or so, where people divide into small groups and discuss what behaviour they want and don't want in the session, such as:

- punctuality;
- confidentiality;
- silent mobile phones;
- respect;
- safety to explore personal issues;
- fun;
- . . . etc.

Usually they compile their small group suggestions on a piece of flipchart, then all suggestions are discussed in the main group and a common set agreed. This is then usually stuck on the wall as a reminder to all.

Maybe I've just been unfortunate, but my experience of this type of exercise from both sides of the coin has been that it interrupts the flow, causes people to focus on potential problems and what they don't want in the session (as well as what they want, of course), delays the real start to the session and generally seems to be more about 'doing the right trainery thing' than anything to do with outcomes, design or learning. It seems also to presuppose that people can't be trusted to behave professionally without a big exercise being made of it first, which to my mind is an unhelpful assumption.

Having said all that, one arena where I think contracting/ground rules does apply is in therapy groups – so if you run those, then I do still recommend that type of exercise.

What I do instead is use a warm-up activity linked to the topic of the workshop, then debrief and set the overview for the day within which I'll mention such things as confidentiality, punctuality, use of mobile phones, etc. Other common 'ground rules' topics such as feeling safe to explore issues and achieving their own outcomes should be part of the design, the rapport built within the group and between the group and trainer and arise naturally during the session.

This accomplishes the following things.

- It acts as an ice-breaker, getting people interacting and exchanging names, etc. without that being the sole focus of the activity.

- It gets people focused immediately on a task and working together, rather than going through a slower round-robin introduction of names/backgrounds, etc.

- It's great for introducing new teams to each other and getting them used to working productively.

- It can double as an 'identity-building' exercise for a new team.

- It's high energy and so gets them used to talking and working, making your job easier in the debrief as they'll have broken the 'training room silence' already and be far more likely to share their experiences with the group.

- They'll be feeling part of a smaller unit, feeling less self-conscious in the larger group and more likely to interact with it than as an individual – again, making your job easier.

My favourite warm-up activities usually involve a set task for small teams. The first two listed below are ones I've found perennially useful.

WARM-UP ACTIVITIES/ICE-BREAKERS

Construction task

Suitable for: Groups of most sizes, in small teams of up to six. Good warm-up activity.

Outline: Set each team a task to 'build' some item relevant to the session, using basic craft materials such as paper tubes, cereal boxes, sticky tape, wrapping paper, card, etc. Ideally, have a box of craft materials per team. Ask them to name it according to the strengths of their team. Have lively background music on.

Facilitator prep. time: Putting together craft box(es).

Running time: 10–30 minutes, depending on complexity of task (usually takes longer than you think).

High energy

Coat of arms/team logo

Suitable for: Groups of most sizes, particularly those that will be divided into teams for duration of workshop/session. Good warm-up activity.

Outline: Each team has a flipchart sheet and coloured markers/crayons and have to design a colourful 'coat of arms' or logo to portray the team values and name. Underneath they have to put a motto (fake Latin allowed!). Have lively background music on.

Facilitator prep. time: Negligible.

Running time: 10–30 minutes, depending on importance of team-forming (longer if teams will be working together for more than a day).

Medium–high energy

Nosy Parkinson

Suitable for: Groups of any size.

Outline: Each person is given a clipboard (or improvise an equivalent) and has 5 minutes to come up with 20 innovative interview questions. They then have 10–15 minutes to 'interview' the others in the room, asking one question per person and recording their name and answer. Prizes (small chocolate bars, etc.) are given at the end for the three (or any number) most unusual questions and the (three) most unusual answers.

Facilitator prep. time: Negligible.

Running time: 15–25 minutes in total.

Medium–high energy

Criterion chairs

Suitable for: Groups of up to 20, space allowing.

Outline: Put enough chairs in a circle for everyone but you (best done before they enter a room, so run after lunch or as first activity of the session). You stand in the centre and call out a criterion for change: 'All those wearing black socks, change chairs'. In the rush to change chairs, you nab one chair. The person remaining calls the next criterion. Rule: no one can return to their own chair in the same go. No need for background music.

Facilitator prep. time: 5 minutes.

Running time: 5–10 minutes.

High energy – use as an ice-breaker, warm-up activity after a break or re-energizer.

People bingo

Suitable for: Groups of any size.

Outline: Prepare a 'bingo sheet' (see Appendix 2) of events, characteristics or relevant criteria, one per person. To lively 'cocktail party' music, have people mingle and interview others, trying to fill in their boxes with names of those who fit the bingo criteria. First person with full house wins, or person(s) with most boxes filled by end of activity wins.

Facilitator prep. time: 15 minutes, plus photocopying.

Running time: 10 minutes.

Medium–high energy

BRAINGYM

This deserves a section of its own in that it's a versatile, energizing and scientifically proven tool that stimulates parts of the brain that other exercises cannot reach.

BrainGym is the marketed selection of a group of 'educational kinesiology' techniques created by Dr Paul Dennison in the 1980s. Educational kinesiology is a system used by physical therapists to improve brain function and motor movement and is backed by considerable scientific research. You can read more about BrainGym at http://braingym.org.uk

Each BrainGym exercise has a specific set of effects on the brain and body and the range offered in the book *BrainGym for Business* by Dennison, Dennison and Treplitz means that you can put together your own short series for near enough any purpose.

You can use the simple exercises in BrainGym:

- as an energizer during 'long-haul' exercises;

- to wake people up after a heavy lunch;

- to prepare people mentally for activities requiring particular thinking skills (e.g. abstract thinking, short-term memory);

- to complement the intelligent use of space to boost mental activity and change energy;

- as a 'hand-around' activity to get everyone involved in fun facilitation – different people lead a few BrainGym exercises throughout the day whenever they want a break;

- as an energizer, opener and tool in meetings;

- wherever you are – there are standing and sitting exercises so location and mobility are no issue.

These BrainGym exercises go down really well with groups and, moreover, improve thinking skills and physical condition.

Suggested format

The way I most commonly conduct a BrainGym session is as follows, though it lends itself equally to more demure applications without music:

- select up to five different exercises according to what I want them to do;

- sequence them from 'safest' to 'most energetic' (for example, Thinking Cap, Brain Buttons, Elephant, Cross Crawl);

- get the group on their feet and in a space if available;

- put on loud, upbeat music;

- demonstrate each move while they follow along in the manner of an aerobics class;

- explain what each move is called and what it does – great for those needing the 'why'.

  Where and when could you use BrainGym?

OFF-THE-SHELF ACTIVITIES

In this section you'll find a variety of activities that are participant-oriented and conform to the whole-brain approach to learning. Each can be used in a wide range of contexts, so you should be able to pick them up and simply insert your own subject matter.

First of all, go back to your template and decide for each section which of the categories below it falls into:

1 information/theory;

2 new skill or skill practice;

3 exploring or reviewing knowledge/learning (new or existing);

4 idea generation;

5 raising or refreshing group energy.

Very broadly speaking, most activities within a group session come under one or more of those headings, and below are a number of generic and adaptable exercises that cover them all. You might want to try them exactly as they are or use them as a basis to create your own.

I have given approximate preparation times as a guide. These will vary according to the level of detail you are comfortable with.

Key to 'Plays to':

RSVP: reason, sound, vision, physical (see pp. 40–2)

MIs: Multiple intelligences (see pp. 42–5)

H&M: Honey and Mumford (see pp. 45–7)

R+L brain: right and left brain (see pp. 39–40)

Activities to convey information or facts

These are usually more heavily theorist/reflector in that most traditional information-imparting sessions favour those styles through an emphasis on passive delivery and large amounts of text. By altering the emphasis from facilitator- to participant-led activity, the activists and pragmatists can be more involved.

Treasure hunt

Suitable for: Small groups/teams, pairs or individuals.

Outline: The information required is presented as a task or quest, then participants search for the information around the room (or larger area) and put it together to present back as a play or presentation to teach to the rest of the group.

Facilitator prep. time: Minimum 30 minutes (write task and photocopy, hide information), maximum 1 hour (design graphics/theme for task/theme, collate and design information or commit to alternative media, e.g. CD/tape, before hiding).

Running time: 30–60 minutes, plus debrief.

Plays to: RSVP, MIs (P, L, InterP, V/S, M if background music used, N if outdoors used), H&M (A, P, T, R if time to take notes after), R+L brain.

Whole-brain rating: up to 14/18

_____

_____

_____

_____

Crossword plus reference source(s) if needed

Suitable for: Small groups/teams, pairs or individuals.

Outline: Participants complete a pre-prepared crossword individually or in small teams, first drawing on their own knowledge of the subject then researching/pooling answers. Ideally make crossword large and multicoloured (team colours for different answers) or get them to create it as part of the exercise. Have baroque music in the background for concentration.

Facilitator prep. time: Minimum 30 minutes (design crossword – but see www.puzzlemaker.com for ready-made crosswords to download), plus location of source material for answers.

Running time: 20–30 minutes, plus debrief.

Plays to: RSVP, MIs (L, M/L, IntraP if solo/InterP if team, V/S, M, P if large crossword on flip/wall/floor, etc.), H&M (P, T, A, R if solo), L+R brain.

Whole-brain rating: up to 14/18

_____

_____

_____

Press conference

Suitable for: Individuals within a large group (the press conference), but could use small group/team or pair preparation time.

Outline: Facilitator holds a 'press conference' on the subject, allowing questions (both primed on cards and freeform) from the 'press' (participants). Brief participants on what notes to take beforehand and what will be handed out in their materials. Get them to assign 'press personalities' to each questioner (*à la* Janet Street Porter) to add humour content. Good opportunity for them to ask their own questions about the subject and could get teams beforehand to prepare what questions they want answered.

Facilitator prep. time: Approximately 10 to 30 minutes, depending on detail/design of prompt cards and assuming a good knowledge of subject.

Running time: 20 minutes maximum.

Plays to: RSVP (if writing and/or standing when questioning), MIs (L, InterP, V/Sish, P if standing when questioning), H&M (A, P, T, R), L+R brain.

Whole-brain rating: 13/18

_____

_____

_____

_____

Advertisement

Suitable for: Individuals, pairs or small groups.

Outline: The task is to create a TV, billboard or magazine advertisement 'selling' either the benefits (applications) of a particular skill, tool or piece of knowledge, or using the skill, tool or knowledge within the advertisement. This is an immensely adaptable exercise, the main purpose of which can be customized to suit most learning outcomes.

Facilitator prep. time: Minimal; enough to set the outcome(s) and source any props needed.

Running time: 20 to 40 minutes, depending on numbers and duration of ads.

Plays to: RSVP, MIs (L, M/L, Inter/IntraP depending on whether solo or in pairs/groups, V/S, P, M, N if using nature as part of the ad), H&M (A, P, T, R if reflective time built in during/end), L+R brain.

Whole-brain rating: 16–18/18

_____

_____

_____

_____

Activities to practise skills

In terms of whole-brain activity, skills practice necessarily errs towards the activist and pragmatist styles in that it's applying a skill. So long as you have a balance of activities that play to all styles over your session, don't get too hung up on making sure each exercise includes them all. Using a more whole-brain approach automatically makes exercises lean more towards activist/pragmatist, so think about punctuating your day/session with opportunities for reflection and providing sufficient information to cater for the reflectors and theorists.

Role rehearsal

Suitable for: Groups of three or pairs.

Outline: Using live situations, have participants practise skills with another, briefing each other first as to the background of the situation they want to rehearse and their partner's role. When using a third person as 'coach', have them observe (a) what went well (in terms of use of the skills being practised) and (b) what they could add in next time. Have them rotate when they swap roles each time so that the roles get 'anchored' to the chairs being used. Be their timekeeper as they'll probably lose track once under way. Play baroque music in the background to aid concentration and give time afterwards for individuals to capture learning for themselves.

Facilitator prep. time: Negligible.

Running time: 30–90 minutes, depending on skills being practised, number in group (threes take longer) and type of skill being practised.

Plays to: RS(V)P (visual input can be added if a crib or feedback sheet is used), MIs (InterP, L, M, P, V/S, IntraP), H&M (A, P, R), L+R brain.

Whole-brain rating: 15/18

Storytime

Suitable for: Individuals within small to large groups.

Outline: When training language-based skills, knowledge, procedures – in fact anything that can be conveyed using words – have participants tell a 'round robin' fairy story (or sci-fi, etc.), continuing on from each other's 'chapter' but utilizing a different skill learned each time or each round. Add in coloured laminated cards with different aspects of the skill that they have to include halfway through, then ring a bell and get them to pass their cards round and continue, etc. Use atmospheric music in the background to complement the story. Optional elements: add in optional 'scenes' that require some acting (a symbol on certain cards, etc.), have them use props to illustrate, throw in random elements yourself to test out their knowledge. Give individuals time afterwards to capture learning.

Facilitator prep. time: Preparation of cards 2 hours if including printing out and laminating.

Running time: 10–30 minutes depending on complexity of skills and exercise stages.

Plays to: RSVP (if acting), MIs (L, V/S, M, P, InterP, IntraP, N (if nature element to story), H&M (A, P, R), L+R brain.

Whole-brain rating: 16/18

_____

_____

_____

_____

Speed-dating/-selling

Suitable for: Small groups in sets of two (four to eight per circle), as many as will fit in the room.

Outline: Great for sales, negotiation, communication skills. Participants sit in two circles, one inside the other, chairs facing so that those in the inner circle are sitting facing their opposite number in the outer circle. Facilitator names the skill to be practised (e.g. negotiation skills) and they have one minute to practise, then the participants in the outer circle move their chairs one person to the left and another skill is practised. Hand out prompt cards to ensure all skills are being practised, not just the favourites. Optional elements: add layers of complexity by doing two or more skills at once, changing the context, etc. Play baroque music in background to aid concentration and give time for capturing learning afterwards.

Facilitator prep. time: Card design time 1–2 hours.

Running time: 10–20 minutes, plus debrief.

Plays to: RSVP, MIs (L, InterP, M, P, V/S, IntraP), H&M (A, P, R), L+R brain.

Whole-brain rating: 15/18

Activities to review learning

These range in duration and style from short, punchy 'wake-up' reviews to longer reviews that are exercises in their own right. Any session should include at least one or two of these to help consolidate the skills and help the memory through repetition. They are designed to help embed and review learning and application, but most can also be doubled up as energizers since they are mostly high energy.

The play's the thing

Suitable for: Groups of most sizes, in teams of up to six; run at end of workshop.

Outline: Teams have 30 minutes to put together a 5-minute play or pantomime of the workshop, covering all the main topics and relevant applications. Provide as many props as possible and, if applicable, get them to do it in keeping with the theme being used. Dressing up, outrageous acting and silly humour should all be encouraged and rewarded. Rules: all must take part, even if it's only narrating. The plays will be performed in front of the rest of the larger group. Encourage them to use music of their choice for their plays. This exercise can produce the most hilarious, creative results and is a great way to end a workshop. It can also be used as a new-skills/information session if added to something like the treasure hunt.

Facilitator prep. time: Prep. of props box.

Running time: Allow 60+ minutes.

Plays to: RSVP, MIs (L, M/L, InterP, V/S, P, M, N if nature themed), H&M (A, P, T), R+L brain.

Whole-brain rating: 16/18

Shape search (mini-review)

Suitable for: Groups of up to 16.

Outline: As part of the room set-up, fix different sets of coloured shapes in denominations that fit into your group number – e.g. four blue stars, four green triangles, four orange circles, four red squares – under the seats (one per seat). At points during the day, get people in pairs or fours to find their counterpart through either colour or shape and explain the last subject to them, ask them questions, discuss applications of it, act it out, etc., etc. Have them re-fix the shapes under different chairs each time. Play baroque music in the background.

Facilitator prep. time: 20 minutes to cut out shapes from coloured card/fix them.

Plays to: RSVP, MIs (L, M/L, InterP, V/S, P, M if playing in background), H&M (A, P), R+L brain.

Running time: 5–10 minutes.

Medium energy

_____

_____

_____

_____

Subject charades

Suitable for: Groups of any size.

Outline: At a suitable interval, divide groups into teams and hand out cards with subject headings on (one or two per person) – their task is to mime an application in the workplace (or personal lives, etc.) for the skill/topic they've learned to their team using the usual charade rules. Should their team not get it within two minutes, it's thrown open to the other teams.

Facilitator prep. time: 15 minutes to write up cards (1 or 2 per person). Alternatively, get the teams to write topic cards for the other teams with the emphasis on topics they want help with applying.

Running time: 10–30 minutes, depending on number of teams.

Plays to: RSVP, MIs (L, InterP, M/L, V/S, P, M, if playing in background, IntraP), H&M (A, P), R+L brain.

High energy

_____

_____

_____

Relay quizzes

Suitable for: Groups of any size, but needs a large room.

Outline: Teams or facilitator comes up with 20 or 30 questions based on the workshop's topics. If teams, each devises questions for the other team. Groups are divided into teams of six to ten, and one questioner per team (ideally facilitators, but if only one then use a person from opposite team) goes to the furthest end of the room. Each team has to send a runner to get the question, return to team, debate and decide on the answer, then send a different runner to give the answer and get the next question and so on until all the questions are exhausted and/or all the team members have taken part. A judge is needed to keep score and make sure no cheating/unfairness occurs (particularly if the questioner is from an opposite team!) Upbeat music in the background.

Facilitator prep. time: 15 minutes to write up questions (make sure answers are known and unambiguous).

Running time: 15–20 minutes depending on team size, number of questions and whether the teams are devising the questions or prepared by facilitator.

Plays to: RSVP, MIs (L, InterP, M/L, V/S, P, M, N if can do outside, H&M (A, P, T), R+L brain.

High energy

_____

_____

_____

Guided imagery

Suitable for: Groups of any size.

Outline: To relaxing music (see pp. 48–51), take the participants through a relaxation exercise, then talk them through the session's learning, with the emphasis on application back in the 'real world', being sure to ask them what they'll be seeing, hearing, saying to themselves, feeling and be doing differently. After reminding them what they've covered, change your style to using more questions than statements. For example, 'It's now a month later, what are you doing differently? What can you see around you? How have you applied what you learned?' This gives each person the freedom to fill in their own experience. After the exercise, make sure you bring them fully back into the room. For example, 'Now it is [date], and you're becoming aware of the sounds around you, the chair beneath you, the temperature of the room . . . in a moment I shall count to three, by which time you'll open your eyes and be fully awake, alert and refreshed. One, two, three.' *NB:* Owing to the relaxing nature of this exercise, it's best to do this before a break and not at the end of the workshop when people might have to drive home.

Facilitator prep. time: You might want to jot down a script for yourself until you get used to the format.

Running time: 5–10 minutes.

Low energy

Crossword (individual or team) without reference source(s)

Suitable for: Small groups/teams, pairs or individuals.

As on p. 98, but this time don't let them look up the answers!

_____

_____

_____

_____

'University Challenge'

Suitable for: Two opposing teams. If teams are very large, nominate individuals within the team to be the 'university team', but all research the questions; the remainder can cheer their team on as the audience.

Outline: Each team has to invent the questions (requiring that they review the material) for the other side. The questions are handed to 'Jeremy Paxman' (facilitator) and then asked of the opposite team. This requires that they review the material twice: once to devise questions, once to answer the other team's. Set the number of questions you want them to produce (suggest around 20 to allow for repetition) and add some of your own for bonuses. Use *University Challenge* theme music, if you can find it, or other game show intro. Have a prominent scoreboard (flipchart) or use physical objects on some kind of track to move along as the score. Ask them to choose a 'buzzer sound' and refuse to accept any answers without it. Can get pretty competitive and hilarious.

Facilitator prep. time: Question prep. time. Choose ones in areas you think they need to review.

Running time: 30–45 minutes, depending on length of research time.

Plays to: RSVP, MIs (L, M/L, InterP, V/S, P), H&M (A, P, T), R+L brain.

Whole-brain rating: 15/18

_____

_____

_____

_____

Info bingo

Suitable for: Small groups/teams, pairs or individuals.

Outline: Facilitator calls out questions numbered according to bingo cards. When the person's number is called, provided he or she can answer the question, that person gets to block it out. First person or team to have a row or full house wins. Play suitable tacky game show music in background. Optional elements: for teams, do jumbo bingo cards.

Facilitator prep. time: Design of bingo card and questions, 45 minutes.

Running time: 20 minutes.

Plays to: RSVP, MIs (L, M/L, V/S, P, M, InterP), H&M (A, P, T), R+L brain.

Whole-brain rating: 15/18

_____

_____

_____

_____

Activities for idea generation

These activities are more targeted in that they're designed specifically to generate ideas by promoting abstract and right-brain thinking.

PlayDoh sculpture

Suitable for: Small teams or individuals.

Outline: Each team/individual has some PlayDoh (and I recommend the real thing, as other cheaper imitations are nowhere near as easy to work with or clean off surfaces) and has to sculpt either a solution to the issue or the issue itself. The more difficult it is to make an easily sculptable representation of the issue (e.g. 'lack of time'), the better. Then they have to build or force associations between the shape and the issue, with a view to generating ideas – stupid is fine at this stage, as it's a creation phase. Use whacky background music (cartoon theme tunes are great) while creating, and get all teams/individuals to feed back to main group at the end to help pool ideas and cross-pollinate.

Facilitator prep. time: Provision of PlayDoh, set-up with group regarding focus.

Running time: 10–20 minutes plus debrief.

Plays to: RSVP, MIs (L, M/L, P, V/S, InterP/IntraP (depending on whether team or individual), M, N (if using natural metaphors for connection), H&M (A, P, (R)), R+L brain.

Whole-brain rating: up to 16/18

Word association

Suitable for: Small teams or individuals.

Outline: Starting with the issue/area for ideas, participants write a list of words that immediately suggest themselves as being connected, however tenuous the link (in fact the more tenuous, the better). For example, for the issue 'time', you could have:

Clock

Tick

Chocolate

Break

Watch

Magazine

Then you go back and, for each word, do a list of associations once again, this time associating to each previous word, not the original. So for 'clock', instead of writing a list of words associated with clock as they did with time, they start with 'clock' and continue from there:

Clock → Grandfather → Old → Antique → Valuable → Sell → Marketplace

Repeat for each of the words, then see what the associations suggest. On the above string, ideas that suggest themselves to me include having some kind of 'time market', where people can buy and sell time in the form of credits for tasks they can't or don't want to do. Use large sheets of paper and different colour pens. Works best with three or four people standing around a table. Have upbeat music in the background, but no vocals as working with words.

Facilitator prep. time: Negligible.

Running time: 20–30 minutes.

Plays to: RSVP, MIs (L, M/L, V/S, P, InterP/IntraP, (N), M), H&M (A, P, T), R+L brain.

Whole-brain rating: up to 16/18

Random object association

Suitable for: Small teams or a small group (e.g. coaching group).

Outline: Have a box, or boxes, of very random objects, such as household items, children's toys, tools, kitchen utensils, craft tools, etc. Get people to pull out an object at random from the box then spend two or three minutes forcing connections between that object and the topic they're working on. Capture on a large flipchart mindmap: have the issue in centre, one main branch per object pulled out, secondary branches for each connection, tertiary branches for any ideas suggested by each connection. Use colours and have non-vocal music playing.

Facilitator prep. time: Preparation of box(es).

Running time: 10–30 minutes.

Plays to: RSVP, MIs (L, P, InterP, V/S, M, N (if natural objects included)), H&M (A, P), R+L brain.

Whole-brain rating: 13/18

Energizers

BrainGym (See pp. 94–6 for full details.)

Suitable for: Groups of any size.

Outline: To lively music, run as an 'aerobics class', with options given to modify any move that's uncomfortable. I usually progress from low- to high-energy moves, using up to five in any one BrainGym session.

Facilitator prep. time: Enough to learn five BrainGym moves.

Running time: Approximately 5 minutes.

High energy

_____

_____

_____

_____

Heel-toe footshuffle

Suitable for: Groups of any size. Fun to run in competitive teams over the duration of the workshop if longer than half-day.

Outline: Teach them (first learn yourself if necessary!) the heel-toe footshuffle basics (see footprints, right) then get them to practise under your supervision (5 minutes, lively background music or none). Later in the day(s), revisit periodically whenever energy is flagging as a light-hearted way of waking them up. If using competitive teams, have the end result a heel-toe footshuffle play-off, where each team has to produce the smoothest and most synchronized movement to music.

Facilitator time: Negligible unless learning for first time.

Running time: Approximately 5 minutes each time.

High energy

_____

_____

_____

_____

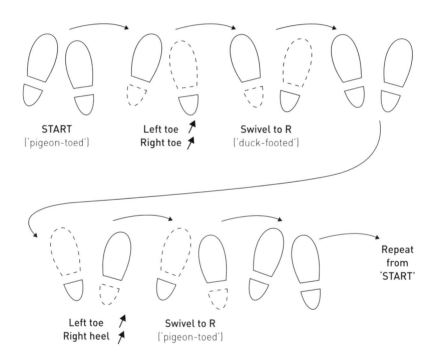

START
('pigeon-toed')

Left toe ↗
Right toe ↗

Swivel to R
('duck-footed')

Left toe ↗
Right heel ↗

Swivel to R
('pigeon-toed')

Repeat
from
'START'

Aim
Continuous movement to
R (then L as get confident)
moving fluidly from pigeon-toed
to duck-footed and travelling as do so

Mexican wave

Suitable for: Groups of any size, especially if seat-bound for any reason (room layout, large seminar/lecture room).

Outline: As per football matches, get the room to do a coordinated Mexican wave – and don't stop until they can do it. Add music to make it more challenging/fun, but not necessary.

Facilitator time: Negligible.

Running time: Approximately 5 minutes.

High energy

Stompish

Suitable for: Groups of any size.

Outline: Stomp is the innovative 'industrial' dance and percussion troupe who drum and dance using only household and industrial materials such as brooms, dustbin lids, oil drums, etc. Stompish is my tribute alternative, using anything to hand in the room, including plastic bags, staplers, flipchart sheets and markers, sweet bowls, water glasses . . . Simply get everyone to grab an 'instrument', then start up a rhythm, nod to the next person to add a different one and so on – until the whole room is bashing away with something. Gets very noisy and is very fun. Add in dance movements if space allows. Alternatively, start it off with clapping and use hands only.

Facilitator prep. time: Negligible.

Running time: 5–10 minutes.

High energy

_____

_____

_____

_____

Criterion chairs

Suitable for: Groups of up to 20, space allowing.

Outline: Put enough chairs in a circle for everyone but you (best done before they enter a room, so run after lunch or as first activity of the session). You stand in the centre and call out a criterion for change: 'All those wearing black socks, change chairs'. In the rush to change chairs, you nab one. The person remaining calls the next criterion. Rule: no one can return to their own chair in same go. No need for background music.

Facilitator prep. time: 5 minutes.

Running time: 5–10 minutes.

High energy – use as an ice-breaker, warm-up activity after a break or re-energizer.

_____

_____

_____

_____

Figure 3.3 gives an example of a more worked up day template. I tend to do the theme and title last, once I know the content. For an example of full facilitator's notes, see pp. 163–5.

Figure 3.3 Progressed day template

AM 1	AM 2	B	AM 3	AM 4
Intro Welcome Warm-up (charades)	**Beliefs** Helpful (audit) Changing them (4-step ex.)	**R** **E** **A** **K**	**Design logistics** N participants Location (dream) Info/learning (conversion ex.)	**Whole-brain learning** 4 main precepts (activity stations) Honey/Mumford (self-audit)

LUNCH

PM 1	PM 2	B	PM 3	PM 4
Whole-brain learning 2 Music (quiz) Energy (BrainGym)	**Building session** Structure (coaching) Timings/breaks (add) Theme/title (creative ex.)	**R** **E** **A** **K**	**Building session 2** Activities (design ex.) Follow-through (own)	**Materials** Theirs (ex.) Yours **Next steps** Projects (commit)

TRICKS OF THE TRADE

This section covers canny facilitation techniques and tools that you can thread through your workshop to make you look and feel like a real pro.

Cunning linguistics

I have no intention of talking to you about grammar, diction, vocabulary or even use of swear words, but I would like to make a few brief points about choices of phrases and how they might affect or enhance your participants':

- ability to pay attention to you;

- level of interest and engagement; and

- ability to comprehend and carry out your instructions.

You can help all this with a few simple choices of phrasing when introducing your workshop, exercises and benefits.

A bluffer's guide to useful phrases is provided in Figure 3.4 and there are more detailed explanations and further examples in the following section on 'Motivation magic'.

Figure 3.4 Bluffer's guide to useful phrases

Situation	Phrase
Introduction to workshop	*Today we shall be covering X, Y and Z [present headline overview and order], with breaks at X and Y and lunch at approximately Z* This gives them an overview so that those who need it can orient themselves
Explanation of exercise	*First, you do X, then Y, then Z – I have summarized it on the flipchart* Set it out as a clear procedure and, if possible, have a visual reminder of the steps so that participants clearly know what is expected
Benefits of workshop/exercise, etc.	*Some of the benefits you might experience are avoiding/saving/putting an end to X or Y [unwanted situation or effect] and gaining more A, B and/or C [desired situation/effect]* This appeals to both types of 'trigger' motivation: avoiding pain and seeking pleasure
When explaining complex or difficult skills/tasks	*This is a very straightforward skill to master once you've practised the steps a few times* Always try to avoid saying 'This is difficult/complex . . .' upfront as it sets up an expectation that it will be, raising an unnecessary mental barrier
When future pacing or getting the participants to imagine using a particular skill or tool	*Think about when you're back in the workplace and applying this: what will you be seeing? What will you be hearing or saying to yourself? What will you be doing – and how will you feel?* (Include the three main senses, plus emotions, to build a vivid and realistic internal image but also to appeal to people whose thinking styles may differ between visual, auditory and kinaesthetic
To get participants more involved with the material	*What's important to you about/in [e.g.] your work?* This connects people with their values or 'emotional hot buttons' in relation to a given context (stating the context is essential)

Motivation magic

Have you ever noticed how sometimes it's really easy to get started on something and other times you have to really 'gear yourself up'? Motivation levels differ according to whether we want to do something or not. What *is* it that 'makes' us want to get started?

Think about the last time you got stuck into a task that you'd been putting off. What caused the final push? Was it an imminent deadline or getting to the point where you couldn't stand it any more or was it that you suddenly clicked into looking forward to the result or what you were going to achieve?

What about when you're learning something new or being briefed on a project? Do you like to have an overview of the subject first so you can place what you'll be doing in context or are you happy to plough straight in and get started on the nuts and bolts without needing the bigger picture?

People differ – that much we all know. In a workshop situation *how* they differ can affect their ability to learn, pay attention and stay interested.

You can affect this greatly simply by the language you use. Below are several sets of phrases demonstrating opposite sides of different motivations. Each is particularly relevant to aspects of running a workshop.

Below each pair is the explanation of both sides of the type of motivation and also a recommendation as to which end of the spectrum to emphasize with your language when facilitating (also represented by the line on the spectrum).

Imagine for a second that you're a participant in a workshop and tick which phrases appeal most to you.

To explain an exercise

❏ 'For the next exercise, first draw a circle, then colour it red, then divide it into quarters.'
Or:

❏ 'For this exercise we need a circle, or you could use an oval or square, divided into quarters. I usually suggest red, but choose any colour that you prefer – and divide any way you want so long as it's into four.'

Procedures ——————————————————— **Options**

If you chose the first one, why? Is it because it seemed clearer? I would have chosen the second. The first is a step-by-step procedure – usually advisable when explaining an exercise, as most learners need to know exactly what and how and in what order, to do something new. However, some (myself included) find it hard to carry out instructions and usually want to adapt them in some way; hence preferring to be given options. If you're like me, your language will reflect that. I had to learn consciously to be more 'procedural' in my instructions as I was confusing people by giving them too many choices in what should have been a simple process.

While usually I'll recommend using both ends of a particular motivational spectrum, in the context of group sessions, and exercises in particular, I recommend you use clear, simple, step-by-step 'procedural' instructions when outlining activities, even if you're the kind who prefers options. It's the better mode for learning, and the options-types will adapt it anyway.

> *For Procedural motivation, use phrases like: 'first . . . then . . . after which' (speaking in a procedure, almost), 'the right way', 'methodology', 'established way', 'process to use'.*

> *For Options motivation, use phrases like: 'several ways you could . . .' 'alternatives are . . .' 'you could also use it . . .' 'a way round it would be . . .' 'choices', 'short-cuts'.*

To introduce benefits

❑ 'This workshop will end those "Monday morning blues", solve the problem of what to do next in your career and save you hundreds in coaching bills, career workbooks and adult education courses.'

Or:

❑ 'This next workshop will give you a clear direction for your career, get you leaping out of bed on a Monday morning once again and have you doing the work you love and getting paid for it.'

Avoid ————————————————|———————————————— **Achieve**

If you chose the first one, you probably enjoy problem-solving in certain contexts and are good at spotting what could potentially go wrong. Over half the working population is like this, so using phrases that tap into that drive to solve problems is useful and they're likely to think 'pie in the sky' if you only talk to them about results and what they'll gain. The second phrase was aimed at those who prefer to achieve goals and gain results. They're not interested in what they can avoid but in what they can achieve and are likely to label problem solvers as 'negative' if that's all they hear.

I suggest that on the sliding scale of Avoid → Achieve, you use both types of phrasing to 'sell' your benefits so that you catch the attention of both types in the audience, unless you know for sure that you have a bunch of problemsolvers (e.g. health and safety types) or goal-oriented (e.g. sales types) as your group.

> *For Achieve motivation, use phrases like: 'get x result', 'gain y', 'solution', 'better', 'more', 'so that I/we can', and anything that points towards an achievement, goal or positive results.*

> *For Avoid motivation, use phrases like: 'avoid', 'prevent', 'stop', 'solve x problem', 'negative consequence', 'don't want', 'wouldn't want', 'otherwise' and anything that indicates something to be avoided or prevented.*

As an opening statement

❑ 'Over the next day we'll be covering: where you are in your role, where you'd like to be, what you need to close that gap and what your next steps are. The first exercise gives you an overview of where you are now . . .'

Or:

❏ 'If you would like to turn to page 3 of your workbook, halfway down there's a five-step exercise that will help you discover exactly where you are at this moment in your role as a team manager. Take ten minutes to answer the first three questions . . .'

Overview ——————————————————————— **Detail**

If you chose the first one, you probably like to have the big picture before going into detail, if you do detail at all. People who prefer this can get lost if you start right into the session with no overview and need the outline so that they can orient themselves and gauge where they are during the session – too much detail too soon and they'll feel overwhelmed. On the other hand, if you chose the second, you might be more comfortable looking at the specifics of a situation and prefer to know all the detail – if you're only given headlines you might feel concerned that you're missing important information.

My suggestion here is always to start your session with an overview so that those who need it can orient themselves, then set out exactly when and where the rest of the information can be found (either in your explanations as you go or in their handouts/workbooks, etc.) for those needing more detail.

> *For an Overview, use phrases like: 'the headlines are', 'briefly . . . (then be brief!)', 'the big picture', 'the overall aim', 'the main sessions are . . .' – and keep your sentences short and your intro punchy.*

> *For the Detail, use phrases like: 'specifically, this will involve . . .' 'going into more detail, we will be . . .' 'what that means exactly is . . .' and use longer sentences. However, spend more time in Overview mode when up front since you can always go into more detail on request.*

When talking one to one

❑ 'I can't tell you for sure that this will work for you – only you can decide that – but if you'd like to try it out I'd be interested to know if it's worked for you . . .'

Or:

❑ 'I guarantee you'll find this tool really useful. Just apply it in this way and you'll see the results in no time. Everyone I've shared it with finds it great for . . .'

Internal ———————————————————————— External

If you chose the first one, this might mean you prefer to decide internally: while you might read up on information, it's *only* information and you'll be the person to make the final decision even if it flies in the face of external measures or opinion. If you chose the second, you probably go outside yourself when making decisions in certain contexts – for example, asking others' opinions, looking for measures of progress, etc.

This is all about where someone's source of reference is: internal or external. When in a workshop, it's usually safer to assume that most of your participants are more internal than external, as using language to suit internally referenced people will also reach externally referenced ones, whereas external language won't influence internally referenced people.

> *For Internal language, use phrases like: 'you'll know when/if . . .' 'only you can decide', 'decide/choose for yourself', 'you might want to consider', 'here's some information to help you decide', 'it's up to you', 'can I make a suggestion?' – assume they will want to judge/decide and that all suggestions from you will be taken as information at best.*

> *For External language, use phrases like: 'statistics show',*
> *'in my opinion', 'if I were you', 'others think', 'you should',*
> *'why don't you', 'best practice is', 'X per cent of Y say' – they*
> *are more likely to be influenced by your or others' opinion.*

NB: It's useful to start listening out for where you are on these spectra – your own preferences will dictate your choice of language and therefore influence your audience unintentionally unless you're consciously aware of and selecting them.

Motivational language is also equally useful in written and marketing materials, so it's well worth including a liberal sprinkling of it to appeal to all types and avoid missing potential sales!

To get people more involved

An effective and simple way to do this is to tap into people's values or, as Shelle Rose Charvet calls them in her excellent book *Words that Change Minds,* their 'emotional hot buttons'. This allows them to engage with the material on an emotional level and can be helpful in finding natural bridges between a subject and the participants' experience or interest in situations where they may not necessarily be wholly enthusiastic.

The question for this is: 'What's important to you [insert context]?' So, for example, if you were briefing a team on the latest customer service policy, you could ask 'What's important to you about customer service?'

This automatically taps into their own feelings, experience and opinions on the subject and engages them at a more personal level than staying at the level of policy. It also provides an excellent starting point for exercises building on ways of improving, implementing or disseminating customer service (etc.).

Try it for yourself – think of a context in which you'd like to explore your values and ask yourself:

'What's important to me in [insert chosen context]?'

Setting expectations

Another way in which your language can enhance and influence your participants' experience is in the way in which you create expectations. For example, compare your reaction to the following:

'This next exercise is pretty difficult, but I'm sure you'll all have no trouble with it. It will give you three ways in which you can't go wrong when closing sales and avoiding customer objections.'

Or:

'This next exercise is simple to master once practised a couple of times and will give you three highly effective ways of closing sales and avoiding customer objections.'

The first prepares the participant for difficulty: already they are preparing themselves for the possibility of failure or getting stuck and, if their natural motivation is also 'Avoid', they probably won't even have heard the benefits of doing the exercise as they'll be straight into problem-anticipating mode.

On the other hand, the second way skips over the fact that it's a complex exercise and presents it instead as 'simple to master'. Even problem-solvers won't stumble over that and it leaves everyone free to hear the benefits of the exercise and focus on those instead.

Of course, whether you say an exercise is difficult or not, some people will always find some exercises hard – using positive language won't avoid all such situations. What it will do, however, is clear the mental path for the majority, leaving them free to discover for themselves whether they find it easy or not.

Positive suggestions

Finally, you could also guide your participants' thinking processes and direct their attention towards useful areas in their minds and away from limited or unhelpful thinking.

For example, here are a few phrases that you might find useful.

- **'This may not be relevant to you, but** [insert benefit]'
  This immediately engages the listeners' attention so they can find out whether it is or not and therefore they're more likely to hear the benefit.

- **'One of the things you might love about** [this session] **is** [insert benefit or highlight]'
  This presupposes that there are many things they're going to love and the use of 'might' allows the more internally referenced people to decide for themselves while the word 'love' suggests a strongly positive experience anyway.

- **'Imagine for a moment you're** [describe them experiencing benefit]'
  This sends their attention inward, as they create an experience in their 'mind's eye' of what you're describing, and the words 'for a moment' both reassure any strongly left-brain types in the room that it's *only* for a moment and also give the mind a moment longer to get into the experience.

If you find these useful and would like to use more of them, a ready stock of similarly adaptable phrases can be found in Salad Ltd's 'Irresistible Influence' cards (see Resources section at the end of the book for details).

Quick wins: attention grabbers

What do you know about your subject that could be turned into a 'quick win'?

By this I mean something that will:

- grab your audience's attention or catch their imagination;
- make them realize that what they're learning (whether they thought they were interested or not) is pertinent to them;
- stimulate their interest to learn more.

For example, recently I ran a workshop that included 'language patterns' – which can be a fairly abstract subject when initially encountered by most people. It just so happened (serendipity) that I had spied the company's Annual Report that morning and, flicking through it, I came across the CEO's address. Scanning it, I noticed that he was demonstrating some lovely examples of two of the patterns I was covering, so I opened that subsection of the workshop by reading them parts of his address and 'translating' what he was 'really' saying before we went into more detail and the exercises.

This opening grabbed the group's attention, made it directly relevant to them (fortunately the CEO was highly regarded) and made them *very* keen to learn more.

So what about you?

- What could you use to kick your session off?
- What is it about your subject that interests you most? How could you use that?
- What common experiences could you draw on to link your subject with your audience?

Group dynamics

This wouldn't be a 'tricks of the trade' section without covering that old chestnut group dynamics.

So what does 'group dynamics' mean? Generally it's used in a negative fashion, when discussing how a group got out of hand or when referring to the fact that there were 'difficult people' in it.

This may be a bold statement, but I'll make it anyway: you can largely control and even eliminate 'group dynamics' with good design.

Why do I say this? Because many of the causes of poor dynamics arise from poor design. Figure 3.5 sets out some of the most common manifestations of 'group dynamics', with some suggested causes, their possible design connections and the solution. Then there are some common facilitator's questions that might also strike a chord.

Figure 3.5 Group dynamics

Dynamic	Possible cause(s)	Design flaw	Solution
Talking among themselves	Boredom Large group so disconnected from facilitator Too much anonymity	Not enough activity or direct relevance to those activities	Frame each section carefully, pointing out what they will gain and solve Ensure sufficient high-energy exercises in order to engage more of their attention Break group up into smaller groups or teams
Refusal to take part	Cannot see the point of the exercise or session for them	Insufficient 'selling in' before the session or during the overview The overview and reasons for attending weren't given in the right language	Find out more about their reasons for attending beforehand Get 'buy-in' through asking what their desired outcomes are upfront Adjust language to ensure meeting all types of motivation
Pointing out what's wrong with everything/why it won't work	Drive to find the potential flaw or risk	Could be heavily 'avoid' in motivation, added to insufficient buy-in	Welcome comments as a way of strengthening your points/the exercise 'Get there first' by pointing out what the potential flaws are in concepts but challenging person to solve them
Moaning about the workplace all the time and lots of off-topic discussions	Insufficient structure or engagement; not enough focus on outcomes	Too much 'open chat' time v. debriefing and focus on application and outcome Instructions not specific enough	Pin down exercises into clear steps with specific outcomes so that group stays focused on task and results Increase small group and/or pairs tasks and add a competitive element to keep focused

Common questions about groups

How do I get the group to take part in discussions? The exercises go fine, but then when we do the debrief they just stare at me in silence – it's really uncomfortable.

Change dynamics/seating of the room, also examine the way you're inviting contributions. 'So, did that work?' is a closed question and isn't likely to evoke much response. Looking directly at someone you've had a good interaction with during the exercise and asking warmly, 'What did you discover during that exercise?' is probably going to get a better result. Also, notice how you're sitting/standing in relation to the group. Perched on a table at a similar height to them makes you more 'us' than 'them' rather than standing at the front of the group and emphasizing the difference in height and position.

What do I do if people turn up late at the start or are consistently late back from breaks?

Start anyway. First, give them the benefit of the doubt and state that you will always be starting punctually. Then *do* start on time as, even if there's only a third of the group there the first time, next time around most if not all will be back on time unless you really don't have their respect at all (which is unlikely if you're running well-designed workshops!)

How do I deal with difficult or aggressive challenges?

Welcome them. Aggression is a symptom of a number of causes.

- Such people may be feeling challenged or defensive, in which case you need to create a safer environment for them.

- They could be naturally 'aggressive' in manner but not in intention or emotion, in which case give them the benefit of the doubt and observe their communication style before drawing conclusions and, in the meantime, respond as though they're making a great point (they probably are).

- They have some kind of political agenda that is probably nothing to do with you personally (unless you have a 'history' with them), in which case let them vent for a couple of minutes then gently draw them back to the process (see pp. 55–9 – 'Bluffer's guide to facilitation').

- They may be 'mismatchers', who naturally feel the need to point out what's wrong with any new idea, etc. and who will kindly let you know at every point why that exercise/approach/skill won't work for them or in that organization. These can be absolute treasures and champions if turned around. To do this, honour their input.

- Thank them genuinely (they usually make a very good point) and then pre-empt them with what could be problematic about each exercise/skill/etc. That approach often kicks in their (considerable) problem-solving skills and gets them solving the issue for you. Alternatively, they'll feel the need to prove you wrong and make the exercise work!

How do I get a group involved who clearly don't want to be there?

Start where they are, not where you want them to be. This is one occasion when it's often more useful to dwell a short time on the problems in the room than going straight into the session. Acknowledge that it's not an ideal or desired situation, but that since you're here anyway you may as well all get something out of it.

Find out the level of resentment and cause – was it lack of information and respect for their time and priorities ('Just be in this room at 9am tomorrow')? Is it a new initiative they don't want to happen? Do they perceive no value to them personally?

A good way of approaching this once you've established the reason(s) for their reluctance is to begin with an outcome-setting activity, inviting them to think about what they want to get out of the session.

First, overview the plan for the session so they have an idea of what's coming up, then, in pairs or small groups ask them to think about what they would like to get out of the session. A useful question to ask is, 'If at the end of this session you could take away one thing that would have made it worthwhile for you, what would that be?'

This shifts their focus away from why they don't want to be there and the past and towards what they could get out of being there and the present/future. It also helps you shape the day so that you can tailor certain activities and outcomes to dovetail more with their individual needs, giving you a real chance to turn the group around.

What happens if an exercise runs over?

If it seems to be an important process for the group and useful discussions are coming out of the exercise, allow it to – if you have to for timings, break and resume afterwards or take a 'working break' and allow the groups to get refreshments as they go. While they're doing that, review your design to decide what can be pulled out, shortened, etc. There's usually enough flexibility in all designs to modify as you go, even if it means redesigning an exercise on the fly to fit a shorter timescale.

If they're running over because of wildly underestimated timescales, then do your best to make it appear deliberate. *Never* tell a group that 'We didn't have time to do X' or 'We've run over time, so I'll do Y'. They don't need to know that you're redesigning frantically behind the scenes and this simply flags up what they're missing (and that it's your fault). The session should always seem to go smoothly and as planned so that they can get on with working with the content and not be affected by the process.

To this end, I never attribute times to the overview of events and I even try not to set what falls before and after lunch. In my head and on my trainer's notes I have very strict timings, but I know that within them there may end up having to be great creativity and flexibility depending on where the group goes. So long as you hit the outcomes of the session, the 'how' should be as flexible as you need.

What about if they're all finishing too soon?

This is somewhat easier, as I've never come across a group that resented being 'let out' early! If you're running too short before lunch or the main break and don't want to pull a later activity forward, chuck in a review session and/or energizer as it will raise their energy, help with application (particularly 'Shape search' or 'Subject charades' on pp. 104–5) and, of course, fill in time.

How can I make sure I stick to the timings when I'm naturally not good at time-keeping?

Delegate that to the group (without, of course, it appearing that it's because you're not good at it!) – appoint one person per team, pair or whole group per exercise to be the timekeeper, another the break-watcher, another the energy-monitor, etc. Allocate roles that help to keep them part of the process and give you plenty of reminders as to where you all are. Alternatively, use a kitchen timer or other alarm and set it for each exercise.

What do I do if some participants want to explore an area or activity further, whereas others have an urge to move on without ending up with two parallel groups?

First, it might not be so bad to have two parallel groups. If there's sufficient flexibility in your material and time, this could be an opportunity for a 'project break' – which is my impromptu name for turning this situation into a process. Set a time (usually around 15 to 20 minutes) and in that 'project break', each group and/or individual gets time to focus on what's currently of most interest to them so far in the workshop. So for those wishing to go deeper into the current area, they can, and others may revisit earlier material or start to examine ways to apply what they've done so far. Your role at this point is floating coach – make your way around the room, ensuring that everyone is using the time productively. It can be helpful to have pre-written suggestions on a flip that you can display for activities they can focus on during the 'project break' to make it look even more deliberate!

If there's no time for such a break, then just rein them in with such an explanation – people will always work at different paces and sometimes that means that there's insufficient time. In such cases I ensure that towards the end of the workshop I revisit any areas 'hanging' for people and help them devise a way to complete the work – whether through buddying with another in the group, a check-in call with me or simply an appointment in their diary with themselves to revisit it.

How can I cater for a variety of culturally diverse expectations? For example, one culture wants expertise and transfer of knowledge, another wants fun (or they sulk), another wants lecture-style workshops and yet another wants long lunch breaks for networking!

In this situation, I'd highlight it and make it a feature of the workshop. It sounds as though you know the different cultures well and can tap into their reasons for the different styles, so I'd divide the day/session into themed or coded 'styles' and play up the underlying benefits so that each feels 'at home' at least once during the time and can also see the relevance of the other styles. So, for example, taking a day workshop, I'd have:

- the whole thing running interactively and perhaps themed around something like the solar system – using a theme to allow the change of style/elements and to satisfy the 'fun' element, but making sure they were totally sure of the reason for the theme to satisfy the need for expertise also;

- have one of the planets – maybe Uranus? – governing a session that was formal in style to satisfy the need for lecturing and to give a frame for it, but top and tail it with interactivity or an energy raiser;

- energy raisers or BrainGym would be governed by/visits to Mars;

- networking lunches and breaks (highlight the purpose of them for those needing expertise) would be governed by/visits to Venus;

- transfer of knowledge and expertise should be implicit in the workshop, of course, but you could do worse than ensure you're citing as many authorities as possible throughout and also making explicit why you're doing everything to further emphasize your own process expertise and give them something to take back to their own teams.

In this way – or your own version of it – you could turn the issues into a feature of the workshop design that reflects, as well as caters for, the diversity and variety that the cultures themselves bring to the table.

How can I make my voice (sound) more powerful, especially at the beginning of the workshop when I am most likely to be nervous and my voice is at its weakest point (for my own confidence and also to make a confident and positive impression on my audience so I can build rapport)?

As I said in the introduction, voice training and control isn't an area I'm covering in this book. Having said that, there are some design tips that could help.

- Do a warm-up exercise/high-energy ice-breaker before you do *any* introductions, so that you, as well as they, are warmed up and relaxed by the time you have to address them more formally. By then any initial nerves have usually disappeared so your voice should be at its normal pitch.

- Have voice exercises (tongue-twisters, mock scales, staged singing) as the ice-breaker, thereby warming up your voice as part of your opening routine – and also reducing your nerves.

- Use the way your voice changes by opening with a metaphorical story that starts quietly or uses different voices, allowing you time to get into your stride and play to the varying qualities of your voice while capturing your audience's attention in a creative and relevant way.

There is, of course, no substitute for the breathing and posture exercises that good voice coaching can offer, but this is how I'd use design to ameliorate or even eliminate the situation.

Everyone talks about building 'rapport' with my audience. What the heck does that mean and how do I do it?

Rapport simply means 'on the same wavelength'. When observed between two people, you are likely to notice similar posture, limb position, breathing rate, facial expressions and they're likely to be deeply engaged in their conversation or happily enjoying each other's company in some other way. Between a facilitator and a group, you are likely to notice a lot of friendly interaction, probably humour, similar facial expressions, perhaps also similar posture and body position where possible. On another level, the facilitator is probably using phrases and words that fit the group members' experiences comfortably and illustrating with examples that make sense to them.

You can build rapport in various ways.

- **Physically** – whether one to one or taking a 'poll' of the majority of the group, try to match their position (you could perch on the edge of a desk if they're all seated), posture (sitting upright or forward, leaning back), degree of eye contact (some like constant and direct eye contact, others need to look away often), even limb position (if most or all are sitting with folded arms, loosely cross your ankles or wrists to match). Don't feel tempted to *mirror* – which is doing exactly the same as the other – as that happens unconsciously anyway when you're in deep rapport with someone and doing it consciously can look more like mimicry. Doing something similar, i.e. matching, is more than adequate.

- **Verbally** – ensure you're using phrases that suit all styles of motivation and thinking styles in the room, not just your own (see pp. 118–128 for tips), include benefits and values that you know are important to the group (see p. 124 for how to find out), and ensure the speed and tone of your voice is similar to the person(s) you're addressing.

- **Design** – not wishing to labour this point(!), if your group is consistently occupied with enjoyable and relevant activities, you'll be in rapport with them by default.

How do I decide what presentation medium to use? Sometimes PowerPoint is appropriate, sometimes not – how can a novice workshop leader choose?

My perhaps unsatisfactory answer to that is: if it's a workshop you're talking about, PowerPoint is rarely – if ever – appropriate. Use flipcharts, walls, floors, tables, 3D models, walkabouts, interviews, CDs . . . anything that requires the audience members to engage with and/or use the medium themselves. If it's a formal presentation, such as a corporate sales pitch, board meeting or lecture to a large audience that would have difficulty seeing a flipchart (though Anthony Robbins uses flipcharts with audiences of over 5000, with TV screens projecting his image), then PowerPoint perhaps is a good medium.

For workshops, however, interactivity is not promoted by the use of PowerPoint unless it's a high-tech backdrop to an exercise (in which case you can probably still make your own wall display and you still have the issue with space needed between projector and screen) and it also adds an unnecessary static and unreliable variable that you could eliminate from your design to incorporate other elements that would also address some of the other issues here. As I've said before, I believe that design is the solution to many common issues faced by workshop leaders, however new or unskilled they are.

People say that the most powerful workshop presenters are those who are being authentic. What does that mean and how can I achieve this for myself?

This is really important and why I often prefer to coach workshop design rather than run workshops on it, as I like to work with the facilitators to find exactly the right style for them as people – and also why I place greater emphasis on design over 'presentation skills'.

To me, 'authentic' means congruent – that is, what you're saying seems to be in line with the way you're saying it, your expression, your gestures, your tone and your behaviour – whether in front of the group, one to one or relaxing during breaks. The easiest way to be authentic is to facilitate workshops on subjects you're deeply familiar with and believe in as the enthusiasm for the subject usually helps compensate for any other concerns about nervousness, being yourself, what the group will think, etc.

However, in the real world, managers, consultants, coaches and other facilitators often have to work with less familiar material for many reasons. Achieving authenticity then comes down to natural style and putting yourself into the workshop.

● Use your favourite subjects or hobbies as a theme – even if the subject matter is not your choice, you can still deliver it in a way that's meaningful to you.

- If you're comfortable coaching but less so up front, make your workshops highly participative and spend more time circulating among your group than in front of it (which, ideally, you'd do anyway with a whole-brain approach).

- Wherever possible, wear what you're genuinely comfortable in and, if you've free rein, allow your participants to do the same.

- Get access to the room in plenty of time and do your best to ensure it meets all your requirements for space, flexibility and light so you can set it up to suit yourself and the workshop in the best possible way.

- Use your favourite tunes to welcome, energize, relax the group and help yourself feel more at home.

STRONG FINISH

Now it's nearing the end: you've designed a fabulous experience, sent out a great Welcome Pack, brought your group together in a well set up room, opened with an energizing warm-up activity, run a smooth, inter-active and successful workshop and it's now at the penultimate activity. You're on the home straight. You can relax.

Wrong. As in the theatre, sessions are never over 'till the fat lady sings'. Keep your eye on the ball and on your outcomes until the last person leaves the room, *then* you can relax. Even if you've run the workshop of your life, it can still all go horribly wrong in the final ten minutes if you take your foot off the pedal – believe me, I know!

So how do you ensure that you finish as strongly as you start? The best way I've found is to use a high-energy, upbeat ending activity that brings together everything the participants have covered/learned and sends them out on a high.

Any of the review activities and some of the energizers are suitable can-didates for the last exercise, but, if you'd prefer to design your own, a good end activity should include the following elements.

- **A strong team factor** – whether that be teams that have run through the session or new teams (often it's useful to mix up the group if they've been working a lot in set teams in order to re-establish the larger group identity).

- **A large dash of silliness and fun** – dressing up, *It's a Knockout*-style games, anything that cannot be taken too seriously while being an effective vehicle for your subject.

- **A cause to review the material** – the end exercise isn't just about having fun and going out on a high; it's also to reinforce the pearls of wisdom the participants have picked up on the way.

- **A whole-brain activity** – it may be that after your session your participants have to drive home or return to work, so the more awake their brains, the better!

What are your ideas for your own end activity?

Future pacing

As well as such devices as real-life projects, project groups, follow-up coaching and peer support, you can also add subtler ways of helping your participants apply the knowledge, tools and skills they've learned in your workshop.

'Future pacing' is a term from neurolinguistic programming (NLP) that means helping people to think ahead in various ways to how they'll be using the material learned, thereby increasing the chances that they'll actually use it (along with, of course, the project and follow-through).

There are many ways to do this, but here are three of the easiest.

- **Using language** – simply by dropping in phrases such as 'So, when you're back at work tomorrow/next week applying these skills . . .' or, more obviously, 'Imagine you're back at work and Y happens, how you'll apply/respond . . .'

- **Using gestures** – generally (*very* generally) people think of the future off to their right in front of them, so when referring to application of the material in any way, gesticulate off to your left (their right) to encourage their subconscious mind to 'place' the application in the future.

- **Using movement** – just as you can use a brown paper timeline up on the wall to illustrate the session stages, so you can use a real (laid out with masking tape or other non-marking tape) or imaginary timeline on the floor. Simply decide on the timescale to be used, mark out where the present is and where, say, three months later is and then literally walk your participants into the future. Once there, you can talk them through what they'll be seeing, feeling and hearing to build even stronger associations in their minds. **Do** remember to return them to the present at the end, though, as some people can become disoriented otherwise.

So, whether you do it casually and subtly or more obviously as an exercise, building in future pacing is another layer you can add to your design that will help your participants translate their learning into application, with little or no cost or preparation on your side.

EVALUATION

Few people actually enjoy this bit, particularly when done as a traditional score sheet (often called 'happy sheet') – neither the facilitators, as they dread a poor 'mark', nor the participants, who just want to go home/back to their desk/off to work after the session and not be delayed precious minutes trawling their way through questions that they put little thought into.

Here I am dealing only with evaluation of your workshop. There are other levels of evaluation, but they get more into training territory. For the purposes of occasional workshops, this evaluation is about: did they get the result they and you wanted and can you learn anything from the experience to feed into later workshops?

Given that so few people relish the idea of post-workshop evaluation, why do it at all? I can think of a number of reasons, but do add your own:

- ensuring expectations have been met.
- comparing your own impressions of what worked and what didn't

with the participants' for the sake of future sessions or personal learning/development;

- handing back to the client to reassure them that you did a great job;

- government/organizational requirement;

How about the following (if you haven't thought of them already)?

- source of business referrals;

- source of testimonials and good reviews;

- potential channel for further sell-on.

So how can evaluation be carried out both meaningfully and enjoyably? Figures 3.6, 3.7 and 3.8 provide three examples of evaluation forms: the first very informal but still informative; the second slightly more formal and results-oriented; the third most formal and outcome-based.

A word about scoring

If you're going to use scores or multiple choices on the evaluation form, as in Figure 3.8, it's often best to use round numbers to avoid the 'stick a mark in the middle' opt-out.

Figure 3.6 Evaluation form: Example 1

So . . . what did you think?

Simply indicate on our thermometer your overall impression.

HOT!

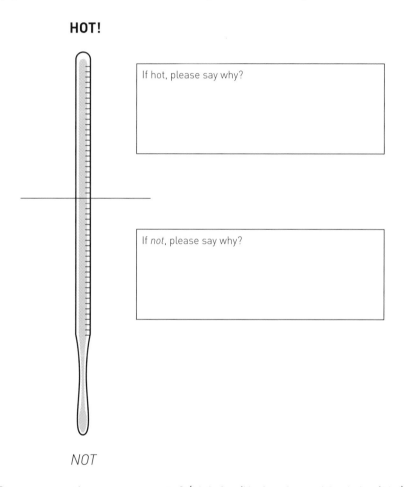

If hot, please say why?

If *not*, please say why?

NOT

❑ Can we use these comments? (*tick for 'Yes' or leave blank for 'No'*)

❑ Can we use your name? Name/title: _____

Thank you for taking the time to join us on [insert name of session]!

Figure 3.7 Evaluation form: Example 2

[Insert session title]

We like to meet our clients' expectations and post-programme feedback is an important contribution to that process. We would really appreciate your letting us know how successful we've been in meeting your expectations.

1 **Business results** – actual or anticipated. Please indicate where performance has improved/is expected to improve as a result of the programme.

Sales:	(£ value)	**Client retention:**	(%)
Productivity:	(%)	**Quality:**	
Other financial:	(£ value)	**Overall profitability:**	(%)

2 **People performance** How did the programme improve the performance of your people, individually and as a team? Please note any highlights.

3 **Thinking differently** Of all the creative ideas resulting from the programme, which will make the biggest difference to your business and why?

4 **Did I/we meet your expectations?** Is there anything I/we could have done differently or better?

5 **How would you sum the workshop up?** Would you recommend it to others? If so, would you mind writing a few words about it that I/we could use in the brochure?

Thank you for choosing [insert your name] as your training provider!

Figure 3.8 Evaluation form: Example 3

[Insert session title]

Thank you for spending a few moments helping to improve and/or maintain the quality of these workshops/this workshop.

Please would you evaluate how effectively the workshop met the stated outcomes [if you prefer, you could use a 1 to 4 score system instead: (not at all) 1 2 3 4 (fully)].

1   Apply a practical tool for identifying areas where time can be liberated.
❏ Fully
❏ Mostly
❏ Slightly
❏ Not at all

2   Explore areas of improvement that will have major impact on time management.
❏ Fully
❏ Mostly
❏ Slightly
❏ Not at all

3   Set detailed outcomes for four areas of improvement.
❏ Fully
❏ Mostly
❏ Slightly
❏ Not at all

4   Identify three steps for each outcome within a three-month time frame.
❏ Fully
❏ Mostly
❏ Slightly
❏ Not at all

6   Set up a support group to share progress and agree first two meeting dates.
❏ Fully
❏ Mostly
❏ Slightly
❏ Not at all

Do you have any comments that you would like to make about how to improve this workshop and/or what you enjoyed most about it?

Many thanks for participating and taking time to complete this feedback.

The only other thing I'll add is:

make evaluation the penultimate – not last – activity.

Send your group out on a high – evaluation, even the 'lite' type, is not an upbeat exercise, so get it out of the way before your last, high-energy activity, then wave them off smiling.

I'm not going to go into any more detail on evaluation, as, unless you're a full-time trainer in an organization, you're unlikely to need any greater detail than the forms provided or your own versions of them.

In my opinion, the main requirements of a useful evaluation (whether by form, poll, survey, discussion or review) are that it:

- lets you know what worked (often an overlooked facet of formal evaluations);

- alerts you to areas that need improvement or even removal;

- builds constructively on your knowledge and experience of running interactive sessions;

- a bonus would be that it also comes up with ways of improving your session.

If yours provides such information, that's all you need.

SETTING THE SCENE ON THE DAY

So your participants have their Welcome Pack, you've now designed a stonking[3] session right up to the evaluation, you're feeling confident about your ability to facilitate it and your subject in general and you're in the building a good hour early, ready to greet them.

What about the room? If you've read and applied 'Location, location, location' you will have managed to secure a decent-sized room with natural lighting and plenty of floor space and will have laid it out in the right style for your needs.

---

[3] Technical term meaning 'high-impact, whole-brain and great fun'. . .

So what else can you do to ensure that your room reflects you and your aims for the session and does all it can to aid you in your pursuit of an excellent workshop?

Heaps. We've covered suggestions for ideal room layout and conditions; here we'll look at that other old chestnut 'visual aids' and the many ways in which you can use the room itself as one, plus the intelligent use of space.

Visual aids

This term (which kind of suggests spectacles to me, so personally I don't use it) means any display or room materials that enhance the learning, theme or experience for the participants.

Often what is really meant is 'equipment': overhead projectors, Power-Point and any other audio-visual media that:

- require the audience to stare at a point that isn't you for any length of time;
- make a background hum, buzz or noise of some kind;
- anchor you to one part of the room;
- involve technology that requires compatibility, cooperation and/or is dependent on a power supply and the gods;
- require dimmed lights or other tampering with room ambience in order to be used;
- require the audience to be predominantly passive because the medium has taken centre stage.

I don't use them in workshops – for those very reasons – and I am willing to admit the possibility that I'm more critical of them than they deserve, but, in over ten years of designing, facilitating and participating in scores of workshops, presentations and courses, I have experienced or witnessed literally *dozens* of episodes of:

- laptop/projector incompatibility/failure/other embarrassing or time-delaying issue;
- overhead transparencies that are badly placed or drawn, difficult to

see, 'hiding' behind the projector head, upside down, otherwise unfit for purpose;

● badly lit rooms so the visual aids are too faint to be useful;

● rooms so dark for the purposes of a slide show or overhead projector that people actually fall asleep during the presentation (which has also gone on too long);

● softly spoken presenters 'drowned out' by whirring equipment.

Yet . . . **zero** episodes of:

● flipchart or other static, non-technology-based room material 'failing';

● outcries from outraged and disappointed participants that all they're getting is brightly coloured wall charts, interactive flipcharts, toys, floor games, high-energy activities and funky materials instead of the much-anticipated PowerPoint show they've travelled miles to see.

So, in the interests of expediency, efficiency, efficacy and your success, I'm afraid I'm going to risk offending sensibilities or expectations (though, to be fair, I did warn you right at the beginning) by not going into the dos and don'ts of preparing slides, OHTs or any other form of powered visual aid. They have their place in presentations, seminars, multimedia shows; but in a workshop there are many other ways to convey your message.

Intelligent space

Now let's turn our attention to what other materials you could use. Off the top of your head, how many different materials might you see in a typical room? Feel free to include technology at this point. Use the illustration opposite as a prompt.

OK, presumably you got as a minimum:

- projector screen/overhead projector screen;
- flipchart/stand;
- posters;
- handouts.

As it was an exercise, you probably also thought of:

- wallcharts/flowcharts;
- glasses/bottles on tables;
- table decorations/toys.

So what else? Did you also think of any of the following?

- Long brown-paper wallcharts depicting information and/or timelines.
- Colour-coded areas or areas marked off on the floor to help people change into a different 'frame' of mind.
- Colour-coded tablecloths for team identity or activity changes.
- Activity stations set up around the room and screened or covered.
- Coloured shapes stuck under people's chairs ready for review energizers.
- Depending on time and resources, wall coverings depicting the theme of the session.
- Floor charts, games or maps leading people to different activities such as treasure hunts and floor noughts and crosses.
- Areas of the room dedicated to different activities or skills, again to help people get into the right state of mind for them.

These are just some of the ways in which you can simply and cheaply dress a room to considerably enhance your group's experience of your workshop. Granted, it does take more time – many books and courses forget to point that out – but the benefits *far* outweigh the additional time cost.

What will it cost you to apply the principles in this book to your materials and session design:

- extra time in material design and room preparation (though if you're using whole-brain learning you won't need any/hardly any PowerPoint slides so you'll save loads there);
- time and cost of putting together an initial 'start- up' kit – some basic CDs, marker pens, multipurpose toys, tablecloths (Poundland and Woolworths are a facilitator's dream for stuff like that), etc.

What you'll gain:

- happier, more engaged participants;

- more of your subject remembered/applied back in the workplace;

- the ability to turn even the 'driest' material into interactive learning;

- a memorable session that's talked about for all the right reasons;

- successful achievement of your and your participants' outcomes;

- more fun, which, of course, means more right-brain engagement and therefore even more learning and recall.

Use absolutely everything

When 'up front' explaining, presenting or facilitating, as well as the visuals you'll have around the room, you also have your hands and feet to emphasize points, reinforce learning and even signal a change of subject or context.

Your hands and feet? Well, more precisely the air, walls and floor space in the room.

With a modicum of thought, you can use the room, floor, walls, tables, chairs and even the air to help your participants:

- pay attention when you need them to;

- change energy levels;

- use different skills or parts of their brain;

- remember the information being imparted; and

- imagine using the skills and information back at work/in their lives.

Directing attention

If you divide the front of the room into floor-parts, you could have:

- an area where you always explain the next exercise (a flipchart is good, so you can point to the summary of steps if necessary – off to their left or centre);

- an area where you talk about applications with the group or debrief and have group discussions (perched on a table, on a tall chair, etc. – off to their right and your left would be good); and

- an area where you predominantly deliver information and require their attention (standing near whichever visual aid you are using – left or central).

Just as we associate red lights with stop, green with go, ambulance sirens with getting out of the way and even queues with waiting, so the brain easily makes associations (also a right-brain ability) that can make learning and group control easier in your workshops.

After seeing you change position a couple of times, even before they've noticed it consciously, they will have made the link between right for discussion/application, left for explanation, central for information (for example). It makes your job that bit easier and their experience that bit more enjoyable and easier to recall.

This is yet another layer you can add to your design that aids your participants' take-up and transfer of learning. After a few times it becomes as natural as writing up a flipchart (but also see pp. 165–6).

Change energy levels

Going back to the 'Breaks' section, I recommend that you have set areas for energy breaks and possibly even review breaks if you have the space. The more you can demarcate the room for different activities, the better for your participants' energy levels, for the simple reason that they'll have to move more during the session.

This beats the traditional 'sit to learn, move for coffee' syndrome and creates more access into their brains for your information to find a permanent home.

Use different skills

If you're working with subject areas that require different skills or processing, use different areas of the room if you can. For example, a subject such as time management requires logical 'left-brain' skills for diarizing and planning, but a degree of 'right-brain' imagination if you're working with setting goals and what they want to achieve through using time management.

Using two distinct areas of the room for these two skill sets helps the participants swap between them and make associations that will enable them to tap into those areas more easily the more they go back and forth. Walt Disney used different rooms for the various stages of his creative process (creative, planning and criticizing), recognizing that it's far easier to move between the very different intellectual functions if you have also moved yourself.

Remember the information

If you use review breaks, and have those conducted in specific areas of the room (or building), then fairly quickly the participants will have built a connection between that location and recall – again, helping their brains retrieve and reinforce information faster.

You could have a 'memory corner' where they always go to test each other between sections, make specific notes to remind themselves or design aide memoires to take back to the workplace. Anything that will help prompt the brain into doing its job quicker and more easily will help them – and ultimately you.

Imagine using the skills back at work

I touched briefly on this earlier in the book, but it's worth paying greater attention to it here.

Stop for a moment and think of a time or an event coming up in the next few months that you're looking forward to, perhaps something you want to achieve. Spend a few moments enjoying imagining it going really well – think about what you'll see and where you'll be, who and what's around you, how you'll feel, what you'll hear or say to yourself – even what you'll smell and taste if that's applicable.

Now notice where you're looking – are you looking slightly over to your right, straight ahead or to your left? Generally (and this is *only* a generalization, so there are exceptions), if you're right-handed you'll probably be looking towards your right or right of centre. If you're left-handed, it's often left or left-centre.

What does this mean for your group? Well, any time you're describing a skill or application that you want them to imagine themselves doing, gesture off to *your* left, which will be *their* right. This places their eyes momentarily in the space that's easiest for them to imagine the future – allowing, of course, for the fact that the majority will be right-handed. Should you have a group that are predominantly left-handed, then do it to your right and their left.

This does not 'programme' them, nor will it compromise anyone whose future is *not* mentally kept in the area you're gesticulating to, so don't get hung up on how many right-handed people you have in your group. However, it is a nice little aid to throw in, particularly if you naturally pace around or gesticulate – you may as well be doing something useful with your hands and feet!

Applying the theory

So, if you know where you'll be conducting your workshop or even if you don't yet have a room but want to design your ideal layout, you might want to use the blank layout sketch on p. 150 and think about where you could locate the various sections of your session and how you could use the room to its fullest potential.

Where you will:

- do the 'delivery';
- explain the exercises;
- conduct the exercise debriefing and discussions about application; and
- lead the energizers;

Also, where they will:

- engage in right-brain activities;
- carry out left-brain activities;
- go for review breaks;
- go to reflect or prepare individually.[4]

[4] It is often a good idea to have a separate area, or even encourage them to leave the room, for solo exercises or consolidation in order to preserve the room energy for group activities.

As ideas, you could do/use some of the following.

- **Mark out different areas** of the floor with masking tape (fine for carpet, but watch it on linoleum or wood as it can stick if down too long) for the energy breaks or review sessions.

- **Have a 'treasure trail' set out** with arrows on the floor or similar symbols.

- **Devise a floor game** and use flipchart sheets for squares or get creative with the Twister floormat (I've used that to good effect as a review exercise).

- **Allocate areas of the room to be used** during the day for different purposes mark them out in some way using furniture arrangement or floor markers (doorstops, masking tape, even windbreaks or screens if you want to keep a work area hidden until in use – also creates curiosity).

- **Relevant posters** – industry, advertising, popular (to which you can add a topical twist), specially designed/printed if you have the resources. Pictures are right-brain friendly, as well as playing to visual/spatial intelligence.

- **Colourful lists** – remember, if using predominantly words (left-brain), adding colour aids engagement of the right brain, as well as involving other intelligences (visual/spatial). Throw in a few symbols wherever possible and use colour-coding if relevant.

- **Graphs and flowcharts** – these appeal to mathematical/logical intelligence as well as theorists and pragmatists. Making them colourful and perhaps adding pictures, cartoons or symbols further brings in the right brain and visual/spatial intelligence.

- **Timeline** – as an alternative to a list on a flipchart, OHT or PowerPoint slide, why not do a timeline of the session on a long piece of brown parcel paper and put that up to walk the participants along. If situated in part of the room other than 'up front', it also changes their focus and reduces the 'them/us' dynamic since you're moving around and among the group.

- **Colour-coding chairs** in some way (ribbon, tied balloons, stickers) to create teams.

- **Using chairs as part of an exercise.**

- **Hiding colour-shape-coded symbols on the backs of chairs or under seats** for review exercises or alternative team grouping during the day (see pp. 104–5).

- **Have fresh flowers/pot plants** on the tables or around the room.

- **Put fiddle-able toys on the tables** to appeal to activists (fidgety) and physical intelligence, as well as adding visual and right-brain appeal.

- **Use colourful tablecloths,** either on the tables where they'll be sitting or on tables around the room set out for alternative activities – in this case, use colour-coding where possible.

- **Theme the tables** (if a theme is being used) with appropriately designed cloths (easy if the theme is one commonly used for children's parties, like superheroes) and accessories (e.g. magnifying glasses, lollipops and deerstalkers if a detective theme).

Now it's over to you. How will you apply these ideas to your own room? Sketch out ideas for your next workshop on the typical workshop room sketch on p. 147.

Finally, be at home

In addition to the above, do anything at all that helps you feel 'at home' in the room. One trainer I used to work with always carried a Tigger or two with her, and I have a particular song I play when setting up a room that gets me in the mood, plus another I use for all my BrainGym exercises that never fails to boost my energy.

So now your room is thoroughly, utterly, totally and completely prepared.

FOLLOW THROUGH

The last person's out of the door, you've collected up the evaluation forms and they're glowing, and you're feeling (rightly) very pleased with your achievement.

What next? Is that the last you'll see of your group?

Hopefully not, if you've factored into your design some kind of application of learning, whether a project or just some kind of follow-up.

Follow-through:

- maintains momentum;
- reinforces learning;
- provides motivation to apply the learning/knowledge;
- increases your organization's or client's return on investment;
- prolongs contact time with your group, giving you a better chance to build relationships and help them;
- vastly improves the effectiveness of your intervention; and it
- shows you care about their outcomes.

For any or all of those reasons, I strongly recommend you consider building in some kind of follow-up as standard, but ideally in the form of a real-life project.

'Why bother?' (pp. 14–18) covers in full detail the ways you can ensure learning is applied but, to recap, here are some effective follow-ups:

- one-to-one coaching;
- telecoaching;
- teleclasses;
- e-mail;
- group session/coaching;
- presentation;
- award ceremony

What ideas do you have for how you might follow up your group(s)?

Materials

Many factors affect the design of materials for group sessions.

- **Client expectations** – what they're used to, what the last person provided when they ran a similar session, what they would do themselves, etc.

- **Participant expectations** – what they're used to, what the best person they've ever been facilitated by provided, what they would do themselves . . . if they ever ran a session.

- **Your own expectations** – what you're used to, etc. . . . you get the idea.

I have four principles that govern my design of materials.

1 **For whom am I designing them: the participants, the client or me?** Sometimes those elements need to be separated out and occasionally removed, but always I find the question useful.

2 **What is the best way of reinforcing the session's learning during and afterwards?** For during, think about the walls, floor, tables, even chairs (as well as flipcharts, posters, etc.). For afterwards, if follow-up, peer support, etc. will do a far better job than printed materials, then don't be afraid to skip or vastly reduce them (see (1)), and put your design emphasis on materials used during the session.

3 **How can I design something that will be used again and again?** So many handbooks and handouts get binned or 'filed', never to be looked at again.

4 **How can I make the materials RSVP?** (That is, utilizing the reasoning, sound/speech, vision and physical channels)?

Materials are used for a variety of reasons:

- to support the participants' learning, even accelerate it;

- to support the facilitator and make their job easier and more enjoyable;

- to support the environment, making it more conducive to the purpose.

These three criteria are useful dipsticks when measuring the worth of materials – save your time, effort and money/budget by seriously considering to what degree the materials you're thinking of producing meet any or all of them.

CANNY MATERIAL DESIGN

Before you set about designing, creating, printing and otherwise producing a fine set of materials for your participants, yourself and your room, it's worth first thinking about how else they might be used afterwards.

You're about to invest a considerable amount of your (and possibly your company's) time, money and brainpower in them, so designing them with an eye to multiple applications makes commercial and professional sense.

For example, could you do any of the following?

- Rework them into a distance or virtual learning tool?

- Use parts of them as briefing notes in other areas of your work?

- Turn them into an in-house – or external – article?

- Compile them into an e-book?

- Use the room materials as displays at in-house conferences or exhibitions or external ones?

- Turn an exercise into a learning game used by the rest of the organization to teach that skill or, again, externally?

- Sell them to other facilitators, agencies or departments?

Break down the key elements of your materials (including any exercises you've created) and see what you can come up with.

Element	How could you rework, resell, rebadge, repackage or redistribute it in some way, internally or externally?

PARTICIPANTS' MATERIALS

Using the body

Those of you who have done some management development or have had any kind of brush with neurolinguistic programming (NLP) have probably come across the concept that we all prefer to learn or communicate through one or more of three main channels:

- visual;

- auditory;

- kinaesthetic (physical – feelings, emotions, movement).

During group sessions of most kinds, the visual and auditory senses are usually fairly well catered for – even in the most left-brain of presentations, we'll have handouts (visual) and be talked at (auditory).

Wherever possible when creating your materials, as well as making them nice to look at and interesting to read and/or talk about, think about how you could also make them good to handle or involve the body in some way.

For example:

- get your participants swapping seats, walking around, moving, using floor games, doing dance or BrainGym activities;

- laminate cards or paper – the shiny surface feels as well as looks great;

- table toys for people to fiddle with and pull about (stress balls are great for this);

- card games or other games involving pieces to handle;

- any excuse to use PlayDoh, poster paints, big crayons, pastels, craft materials in an exercise;

- rather than using paper or overheads, use walls and have people walk along a 'gallery' or display of information – you can accompany them with music.

. . . and so on.

What else can you think of that would work in your session?

Handouts and handbooks

With these materials, as with the content, less is often more.

Have you ever come away from a course, workshop or presentation clutching a handful or even a ring binder full of handouts . . . only to put them on a shelf never to be referred to again?

Of all the courses I've been on, many of which have been for professional advancement or even qualification, I would say there are only two binders I still occasionally refer to. The rest finally got thrown out a few months ago after literally years of dusty storage.

Having said that, some people do have a need for materials, whether or not they will use them – they're a kind of comfort factor that 'proves' they've either been on, run or commissioned a 'proper' course. If that happens to be your client or boss, then you'll either have to persuade them otherwise – using arguments for whole-brain learning that fewer but more carefully put together materials will actually give them a greater return on their investment – or knuckle down and produce the materials required to satisfy them.

Participants are more easily persuaded. Once they see the materials they're usually more than happy to swap something that would just take up space on a dusty shelf for some funky cards or notebooks that do the same job in half the size or time.

So what are the key principles of learning/support materials design?

1 **Less is more** – what is the shortest, fastest, fewest-paged route to giving your participants the reinforcement they need to ensure they both remember and apply the subjects covered? Think:
   - stickers;
   - business/credit cards;
   - postcards;
   - A5 binders;
   - sticky notes;
   - bookmarks;
   - magnets;
   - games;
   - customized playing cards.

2 **Whole-brain friendly** – how can you make the materials stimulate their reasoning, speech (internal or external), visual and physical capabilities – and both sides of the brain? Examples:
   - use colour;
   - make them tactile;
   - use graphics;
   - link them to teleclasses/-coaching;
   - adapt family games;
   - turn into card games.

3 **Cost-effective** – what kinds of material can be produced, and reproduced, cheaply and easily? What resources do you have access to? Cheapest:

- postcards;
- sticky notes;
- business cards;
- A4 – use graphics as well as text; colour makes it expensive.

What ideas do you have for your own materials?

YOUR MATERIALS

Materials aren't just for participants: there are plenty of materials that can make your life easier and more fun – and, of course, your facilitation more effective.

I have four main groups of materials that I consider essential facilitator support.

1 **Facilitator's notes** – outline of the session, timings and exercises.

2 **Flipcharts** – one pre-prepared, one blank.

3 **Music player/music** – whether portable CD player/CDs or iPod and speakers.

4 **Miscellaneous box/bag/case** – room materials, the essential (and always scarce) Blu-Tack, marker pens (always keep a box of new ones with you – Berol pens come in bright colours), spare flipchart pad, participants' materials.

Facilitator's notes

As I often get asked what I use for facilitator's notes, I've reproduced part of a recent set on p. 166 so you can see to what level of detail I go.

In addition to those, I always have an outline of the day in the form of a mindmap – and often I'll work only from that in the end – see overleaf. The detailed notes help me get the session into my head first and are

Figure 3.9 Mindmap of a great workshop

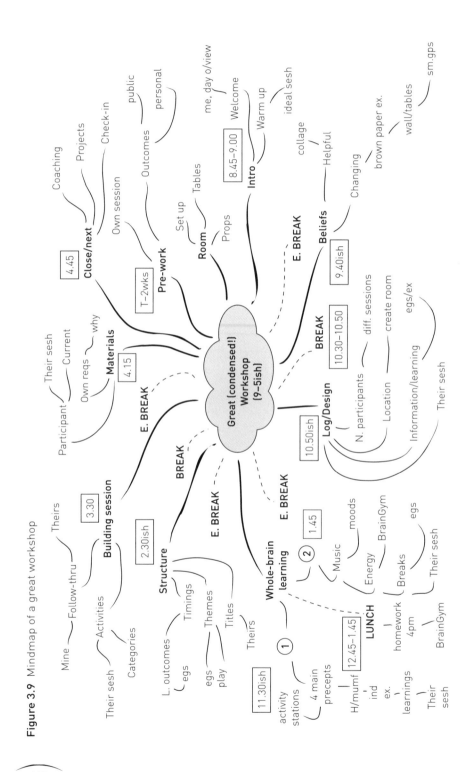

useful to come back to as a reminder of what I did if I run it again. I'll also make notes of any changes to the running order or exercises as I run it so that I can incorporate those later.

As with all the materials in this book, should you want a copy of the file, drop me an e-mail[5] and I'll send it to you.

Example: Facilitator's notes

Innovation in Business

(Not actual title)

Room layout

CD player and CDs

2 x flips   one pre-prepared
                 one 'live' for writing on/instructions

Cabaret table layout

4 x activity stations (RSVP)

Plenty of wall space for bridge exercise

Toys box – clapperboard, paper, craft items, PlayDoh

Inventors' journals [for participants to write their own notes to support the reminder cards]

Reminder cards [a set of full-colour postcards with the key learning points]

Posters – inspirational, thought-provoking, metaphorical

Natural lighting

Space to move about in

Tablecloths

Bottles of water on tables

Things to fiddle with on tables

▶

[5] nikki@metaphizz.com

Day in detail: 9.30am to 5.15pm

Time	Activity	Process	Materials	Notes
9.15am	Welcome	Meet 'n' greet on arrival, allow to look round but no peeking under tablecloths – build expectations	Posters with positive pre-suppositions Intriguing pics if poss RSVP stations x 4 set up (table-cloths over them) with instruction laminates Inventors' journals Refreshments 'Welcome' flip	Room set-up – posters, tables with activities, music playing, cabaret tables
9.30am	Start/intro	Very brief 'Hello, I am . . .' then straight into creative warm-up		
9.35am	Creative warm-up	Each table has to come up with a 'silent movie' with subtitles depicting their interpretation of 'Success' Hand out inventors' journals Debrief – see Notes, right	Blank paper for subtitles Clapperboard and chalk Director's megaphone Inventors' journals	Implicitly getting them to (a) use RSVP (explain after the next exercise) and (b) let us know their collective definitions of success to feed through Debrief: Explain why using
10.00am	Full intro	What this is all about and why do it – see Notes, right Guide on materials: why and how to use them	None	Stimulating more of their brains Reminding them of how creative they are Concrete tools to use in business Technique to access natural creativity Applying the tools to a live situation and supporting them through it End of today: exercise where not only will they learn how Disney made his millions, but also be able to work up an idea to take back and implement, so might want to be thinking about that as go through the day
10.10am	Using RSVP	Brief intro to whole-brain learning Each table go to a RSVP station 10 mins each table to do/		

Time	Activity	Process	Materials	Notes
		read/ learn activities then change (40 mins) 5 mins to perform last activity to whole group (may dump if short on time) Hand out reminder card(s), then additional 5 mins to write up any notes want, in addition to cards Debrief (10 mins) – see Notes, right	Reminder cards RSVP flip	Debrief: Find out how it went, what learned, then re-explain creative warm-up At school, conditioned to value only left-brain activities, but *all* of the brain is used in creativity – as a result we often play down the right side, especially if ended up in biz In biz, mostly left-brain activities: linear writing, thinking, figures, logic, analysis; we waste half of our brain's capacity Can also use RSVP techniques to liven up – and make more effective – meetings, presentations etc.
11.15am	BREAK		Upbeat music	

Flipcharts

What I do use is flipcharts when needing a site to illustrate a point, overview the session, convey clear instructions or capture ideas floating in the room. Generally I have at least two flipcharts on the go: one 'live' and one pre-prepared.

The 'live' one I use for:

● capturing group ideas during debriefs;

● doing sketches or diagrams to illustrate impromptu points;

● handout sheets for exercises;

● sticking up on walls, etc.

The pre-prepared one is a little neater, as I will have written it up before the workshop on a table in my 'best handwriting'. It will contain things such as:

● the 'Welcome' sheet (usually a badly drawn cartoon and the title of the workshop);

- overview of the session;

- summaries of certain key points;

- instructions for certain activities;

- models I'll be explaining, etc.

Flip tips

When using flips, here are a few tips I've found useful over the years.

- If you want to draw something in front of the group neatly, outline it softly in pencil before the session when you can take your time and get it looking right. Owing to the nature of the paper it will be almost impossible for anyone but you to see, and you'll look very professional as your marker confidently sweeps across the sheet!

- If you want to avoid continually looking down at your training notes, use the pre-prepared flipchart as your timetable by preparing one headed sheet for each section and/or exercise in the correct order – you can even mark those just before breaks with symbols to remind you and pencil the timings in the corner.

- To find previous sheets quickly, mark them with a small sticky note at the edge like an index tab, then you can grab that and flip to the page quickly and smoothly.

- Should you want to index more than one sheet (I sometimes index every one if I know I'm going to be toing and froing between them), label each sticky note, again with pencil, so you can see it but your group can't.

- When doing your intro and/or welcome, softly pencil your key points on the corner of the sheet nearest you. You can stand by or even lean on the chart informally while having 'prompts' to hand and, again, your group won't suspect a thing.

- To write in a straight line across a flipsheet, practise the feeling of writing with an upwards slant – you're not actually writing upwards, but if it feels that way you're more likely to end up with a straight line.

- When getting to the bottom of a sheet, to avoid bending or crouching awkwardly, simply slide it upwards keeping the bottom edge parallel with the bottom of the pad, anchor it with your non-writing hand and continue writing. It looks professional and is easy to keep a straight line as the sheet is then raised to shoulder height.

- If you know you're going to be running the same session numerous times, it's sometimes worth having a set or two of laminated flipcharts printed to save you continually redrawing them and for a more professional look. Shop around for printers that do outsize printing to get the best price.

- Buy recycled paper whenever possible – it helps ameliorate the amount of wastage and, for some reason, the perforations seem better on recycled pads.

- If you have a choice, get a flipchart stand that is (a) light to carry around for ease of mobility in the room and (b) the 'flipover' type that anchors the flipchart, not the individual screw-in type.

I'm no artist, so what I lack in flipchart drawing skills (and believe me I do – one public workshop I ran started with a puzzled audience trying to work out why I'd drawn a willy on the Welcome flipchart when it was actually a lighthouse – the metaphor I was using for career change!), I try to make up for with colour and basic symbols. It's a phenomenally useful skill to be able to draw when using a whole-brain approach to work-shops, since well-applied cartoons both on the flipcharts and around the room are immensely useful when designing creative materials, learning aids and for theming purposes.

Generally, though, I use more wall, floor, table and exercise-based mate-rials than anything 'up front', whether that be flipchart, PowerPoint or overheads. Taking the onus off the front of the room automatically reduces delivery time and therefore increases interactivity and partici-pant-oriented activities.

Music player/music

See pp. 48–51 for ideas on what kinds of music to play and when, but as a basic 'starter pack', you might want to have:

- a couple of classical albums – Bach's Brandenburg concerti, baroque compilations, etc.;

- a couple of 'summertime' CDs with classic 'feel-good' songs on for refreshment breaks and music to have in the room on arrival;

- a couple of upbeat dance albums for energizers and any high-energy creative exercises;

- a couple of theme tune CDs, whether classic TV tunes or films, or on specific themes (e.g. sci-fi music, Western music);

- some favourite songs/albums to get you in the mood while setting up the room *that you don't mind becoming associated with work* – this bit's important, because after a while of using them they could become irrevocably associated with work whenever you hear them 'outside'!

Equipment case/bag/box

After you've facilitated a few whole-brain sessions you'll find that you have a few indispensibles that you like to have with you every time. At this point it's worth commandeering or investing in a dedicated carrier. I've got a wheely-soft-suitcase-thing, or WSST (stop me if I'm getting technical), but then my need is probably greater given that facilitation is one of my main roles.

To give you an idea, in the WSST all the time live:

- Blu-Tack, and plenty of it;

- multicoloured sticky-notes, heaps of them;

- several boxes of multicoloured markers (not just the red, blue, green, black standard ones);

▶

- several tubs of PlayDoh (and it does have to be that brand – cheaper ones mark tables, get on clothes, deteriorate more quickly and don't smell as nice);

- loads of CDs that I play only when facilitating (TV/film theme tunes, upbeat dance compilations and albums, 'easy listening', a couple of favourite albums, jazz, classical – mainly baroque);

- miscellaneous pocket money toys for fiddling with on tables and using in impromptu games;

- noise and/or music-making implements for exercises, games or timings;

- spare paper and pens;

- coloured tablecloths – brightly coloured wipe-clean paper or plastic;

- a Twister mat, just in case!

Added to it each time I use it are:

- a CD player;

- room materials relevant to that workshop/theme;

- participants' materials;

- pre-prepared flipchart (I don't use overhead transparencies or PowerPoint, for reasons outlined earlier).

 What would you pack in yours?

4

Meetings makeover

It should go without saying that all the principles in this book apply equally to meetings as to any other group session. However, meetings also deserve a special mention of their own, since they're the poor relative of group sessions and usually sorely neglected in terms of design, materials and interactivity.

Yet they can easily be just as rewarding, enjoyable, interactive and valuable as the best workshop. Imagine if all of your meetings were looked forward to, participated in equally, resulted in measurable results and/or changes and were a resource of skills and information in themselves.

They can be. With just a few simple principles delicately applied, you can turn your meetings into events that are eagerly anticipated and enthusiastically eulogized. Well . . . made more productive, at least.

Reboot the image

Sometimes meetings can fall into a bit of a rut or cease to be very productive. If this is the case and you'd like to 'reboot' your meetings image, here are some ways to do this.

● Change the venue, therefore removing the link between room and behaviour – find a room or location your team has either never met in or has positive associations with.

● If you can't change the venue, change the appearance and layout of the room – anything to break associations with 'the usual' and help people move into a new set of expectations and behaviour.

- It goes without saying that it's *very* important that you also change the running style of the meeting – otherwise you'll simply build a negative association with that location or room appearance too.

- Add in any or all of the following elements to alter the energy, style and results.

Have a clear structure

In order to keep to time, ensure you cover all topics and reach a satisfactory ending with all outcomes achieved, it's as important for meetings to have a good structure as it is for workshops or any group session.

To keep it really simple:

- take the total time allocated;

- divide into that the total number of topics/items to be covered, plus 2 extra slots;

- insert the necessary break(s) if the meeting is to run over 45–60 minutes;

- this allows an opening session, equal time for each topic (you can of course alter that according to priority), plus a closing session – having the closing session as long as any other allows a little time flexibility in case of overrunning.

When running the meeting, ensure that someone is appointed timekeeper (not the person on 'divert alert', below) to flag up when there's five minutes to go to aid timekeeping and also to ensure adequate time to summarize the key points agreed and any actions before moving on to the next item.

Set outcomes

Whether at the beginning of the meeting or before (as part of the Welcome Pack pre-work), set clear outcomes for the meeting and agenda items so that you all know once they're achieved and can then move on.

In addition, have someone on 'divert alert' – make it light-hearted and give them a flag to wave or a beeper to squeak, but at all times have some-one (it can be different for each item to ensure everyone gets to partici-pate) responsible for concentrating on process rather than content and flagging up whenever the topic strays off or gets unnecessarily bogged down in detail or irrelevance.

You'll probably find there are people in the team better at focusing on process over content than others and it may be worth asking them to hold this role more often so long as they're involved in discussions fully whenever they need to be.

Send a Welcome Pack

Just as it's helpful to 'warm up' participants before a workshop, so it is for a meeting – arguably more so, since it's usually of shorter duration. So why not use a Welcome Pack? Particularly if meetings have fallen into something of a rut or are not as productive as they could be, this signals that something different is to come and helps alter their assumptions.

You could include:

- the agenda, of course – better still, make it colourful and creative (and see 'Add a theme', below);

- venue/directions – you could make a joke of adding directions to a room they know perfectly well;

- short preparatory work – something you want them to read before the day (reduce information overload during the meeting), an idea or concept you'd like thoughts on, something new you'd like them to research and précis.

Add a theme

Why not add a light-hearted but creative element to the meeting? Nobody said meetings *had* to be serious, yet most of them are treated that way. Theming your meeting regularly – and you could rotate responsi-bility for it – could introduce a layer of creativity and even development.

It's probably best to do this no more than monthly to keep the idea 'fresh' enough to be useful.

Ways to 'work' a theme.

- Request that the theme is relevant in some way to current work or projects and challenge the theme-setter to demonstrate the links, encouraging right-brain and 'out of the box' thinking.

- Incorporate it in the Welcome Pack – visually in the design, play on words, ask that everyone brings something related to the theme to wear or for the room.

- Use it cross-departmentally – challenge visiting 'guests' or departments to set a theme.

- Link it to current initiatives – as a creative exercise, force connections between the month's theme and any team or organizational initiatives.

Keep the energy up

Energy can flag in meetings just as it can in workshops, so this is an important element to be aware of. Keep agenda topics short, incorporate energy and/or refreshment breaks, introduce activities and exercises rather than relying on discussion for all topics.

BrainGym is a great way to do this and is as relevant to meetings as it is to workshops, given that it was designed specifically to stimulate specific areas of the brain. You could rotate responsibility for running the 'BrainGym-break' – the book *BrainGym for Business* lists various exercises to do under different headings according to business requirement, though it's just as easy to read through the exercises and choose for yourself.

Use music

Have music playing at the beginning of the meeting to greet people as they arrive, use it during the breaks, use it for BrainGym . . . try it and notice the change in atmosphere and attention levels – it can transform a dull grey session into a multicoloured fiesta (or thereabouts).

Most important of all, it's not 'meetingy', therefore automatically shifting people's mindsets slightly and preparing them for something more inter-active.

Make it interactive

Meetings are predominantly to discuss, share and agree items of common interest to a team or group of some kind, but how else could you cover these items other than by discussion? Here are some ideas.

- **Information to share** – send it out beforehand, read it as a 'news bulletin', display it on the wall for them to read at the beginning with music in 'art gallery' style. (see pp. 30–4 on the ways in which you can turn information into learning.)

- **Team updates** – how about having a 'rogues gallery' where underneath a photo of each team member they add that month's/week's highlights? This could be displayed on the wall or sent out as part of the Welcome Pack. Alternatively, use the 'news bulletin' format or have them turn their updates into TV adverts 'selling' their projects to the rest of the team or design update posters . . .

- **Items to agree/discuss** – wherever possible, send these out beforehand to give people a chance to formulate some thoughts and add questions as prompts. You could also ask pairs or small teams to consider different aspects of an item to share back to the group, multiplying the brainpower and involving intrateam work beforehand. Encourage them to feed back interactively.

- **Minutes** – instead of one person taking the minutes and sending out a dry summary of the meeting, how about compiling a group mindmap as the meeting progresses, with each agenda item a separate branch, with a set different colour (I use red) off that branch detailing the actions and times – this could then be photocopied and sent out (in colour if possible).

- **Visiting expert** – how about having each of your team in rotation acting as a 'visiting expert' for an area of interest or expertise they'd like to share with the team. Have them present it in a way that's interactive and intended to share a skill – with the focus on application at work, though the skill certainly – even ideally – doesn't have to be work-based. For example, people have shared skills such as meditation (great for stress management at work), cartoon drawing (great for illustrating materials and flipcharts), photography (team newsletters, in-house marketing), even feng shui (incorporated into an open-plan office). This can really inject an element of interest into a meeting, as well as developing team skills in a way that's creative and innovative.

So there you go – a few choice ways in which you can turn any meeting into an engaging, stimulating and productive use of everyone's time.

Adieu

Well, that's it! I hope you found this book useful – whether you used it as a pick 'n' mix counter or went through it more systematically as a process for design.

Now it's over to you to put into practice those nuggets you liked best, and to reap the indubitable benefits. When you look back in a few months' time on how easily you integrated the various tools into your day-to-day work and group sessions, I hope you will be surprised how much you enjoyed the process of implanting them and how much more you now get out of working with groups in any context.

Until next time . . .

Appendix 1

Some themes suitable for workshops

Theme	Examples of subjects[1]	Implicitly conveyed . . .	Care with . . .
Pirates	Multiple uses, especially change-oriented subjects Boring or 'dry' subjects (insurance [sorry, guys], health and safety, HR procedures, etc.) Theory-heavy subjects (compliance, FSA, etc.)	Daring Swashbuckling Adventure Resourcefulness Ability to use what they have/find Adaptability Survival through tough conditions	They're officially usually the 'bad guys' Very male dominated Not exactly considered 'sensitive'!
James Bond	Innovation Entrepreneurial and *intra*preneurial skills Influencing skills Problem solving Theory-heavy or 'dry' subjects[2]	Resourcefulness Ability to charm anyone (mostly!) Working innovatively but *within* a system (the government) Always wins in the end The 'good guy' Lots of gadgets that can be adapted to use (good for tools learned in the workshop)	Male dominated (but I have used 'Jane Bond'), and he does seem to be a universally admired character
Star Trek	What can I say? *Star Trek* is perfect for anything (or is that just me. . .?)	Model of humans evolved beyond material concerns Equality of all rights Communication issues resolved (largely) People valued for what they contribute Diversity honoured and integrated Exploration Lifelong learning Anything is solvable (just about) Even death is not necessarily the end Technology and human intellect combined Mental evolution to telepathy/empathy	Can't think of any caveats other than some woefully misguided people hate *Star Trek* (you know who you are)
Mission Impossible	Change programmes, and anywhere there is likely to be some resistance Theory-heavy or 'dry' subjects	The Mission is not Impossible at all Good guys always win Adventure Great gadgets (translate to workshop tools) Courage and skill Can always turn a bad situation around	Male dominated again Important to make conscious, and emphasize the transition from, 'impossible' to 'possible'

▶

Theme	Examples of subjects[1]	Implicitly conveyed . . .	Care with . . .
Cluedo	Problem solving Logic-based or left-brain subjects[3] Communication styles Personality profiling Theory-heavy or 'dry' subjects	Deduction and logical processing usually gets to the answer Problem solving can be a game	It's about a murder(!) Slightly limited in application, but I have used it to good effect with communication/personality styles, eliminating the 'murder' aspect
Meccano/Lego	Left-brain subjects Subjects that seem very complex and 'bitty' initially or which take a while to get to grips with Theory-heavy or 'dry' subjects	What can seem like a heap of useless bits can be used to create infinite things	
Hawaiian	'Lighter' subjects, e.g. certain soft skills, simpler practical skills or systems Theory-heavy or 'dry' subjects	'Holiday' feeling, so great for mood lightening and positive associations Ease and simplicity Friendly and positive Add a dash of *Hawaii Five-0* and you have 'good guys' always winning out	Ensure it doesn't become more 'beach party' than learning session!
Literary	Communication skills, particularly more advanced written ones (copy writing, editing, writing, etc.) Just about any subject if you include all well-known works of fiction/ stories Hero's Story (perennial hero + challenge + 'calling' + quest + personal growth + revelation/change) almost infinitely adaptable to personal and professional development subjects Theory-heavy or 'dry' subjects	Skill Elegance of written word Effective communication Timeless fame and renown Influential words (e.g. Shakespeare) Depends on story/work of fiction chosen	If you have a literary bent, bear in mind that your favourite author might not be everyone's (I'm a Jane Austen fan, but she's not everyone's cup of tea so I'm still waiting for the right opportunity to use her), so stick to very popular authors and works of fiction that ideally have been made into films
Marketplace	Great for multiple-skill workshops – you can have a stall per skill/ exercise Good for teambuilding or teamworking subjects as the trading side can be well utilized Entrepreneurial/ intrapreneurial skills Sales, marketing and negotiation skills	Everyone can buy and sell Bartering and negotiation can be learned Presentation is all Success, influence, etc. aren't necessarily linked to position or education Anyone can be a 'self-made man'[4] Anyone can set up a stall Competition is healthy and can be fun	Might need a lot of setting up if going for a true marketplace look Need to ensure any competitive element is used positively

▶

Theme	Examples of subjects[1]	Implicitly conveyed . . .	Care with . . .
	Theory-heavy or 'dry' subjects		
Superheroes	Either alone (e.g. Superman, Catwoman) or as a general theme, great for helping to 'install' new skills Theory-heavy or 'dry' subjects	However ordinary people seem, there could be a superhero hiding inside Never judge a book by its cover The good guys always win (well, usually) Good for linking to greater causes (saving the planet, etc.) Gadgets/powers = tools/new skills Depends on characters used	Can be seen as either silly or non-credible if overdone or done badly
Magic/magician	Subjects that can seem impossible or where there's resistance Works well with lighter subjects that involve some personal change, e.g. presentation skills Theory-heavy or 'dry' subjects	Anything's possible The arcane becomes known; secrets unveiled Sleight of mouth and hand can be learned, therefore magic can be learned Skills can seem like magic	Care with use of magician/wizard as an identity as can seem patronizing if too 'child's birthday party'

[1] Though these are to give you examples of how you might use each theme, I appreciate that there is a definite soft skills bias to the subjects, simply because that's my field. *Je m'excuse.*
[2] You will notice that I've put this use for all of the themes. This is because theming is one of the best ways I know of getting across a lot of theory or a boring subject effectively – i.e. without boring the pants off the participants and with a chance that they'll remember some of it beyond the minute they leave the room.
[3] See pp. 39–40 for a full explanation of left/right-brain attributes.
[4] Sorry, but 'self-made person' just doesn't sound right, and I'm both female and feminist(ish).

Appendix 2

People bingo

Find someone who . . .

Had a chopper bike as a child	Is a Virgo	Loves peanut butter	Wanted to be an astronaut	Has more than one pet	Loves the colour purple
Won't swim in chlorine	Has seen Shirley Bassey live	Sings in the shower	Flunked maths spectacularly	Is superstitious	Has been to a karaoke club
[Fill in your own]					

Appendix 3

Glossary and 'trainer speak'

These are the words you're most likely to come across either here or from other people when referring to training and workshops. Some I don't use as I find them a bit *too* trainerspeaky, but you might want to or have to deal with others who do.

Buzz groups – small groups of between three and six (usually) set to discuss something quickly, then report back.

Contracting – similar to ground rules, but with a more 'official' feel to it owing to the term 'contract'. Often additional element is what the facilitator will agree to do as their part of the 'contract' for the session.

Debrief – the discussion after an activity that covers how it went, what came up/was learned, and how the learning will be applied. Arguably the most important part of an exercise.

Ground rules – an introductory activity that involves people discussing and agreeing on set behaviours for the session, such as confidentiality, punctuality, respect, safety, listening, etc.

Outcomes – what people want to achieve, to greater or lesser detail, whether from an exercise or attendance at a session – for example, a more formally structured 'goal'.

Plenary session – any whole-group discussion or activity, usually the debrief or general discussion.

Session or interactive session – in this book, 'session' means any interactive event you're planning to run, whether that's a workshop, seminar, presentation, meeting, group coaching or party. The principles in the book apply to all.

Syndicate groups – small groups of between three and six (usually) working on tasks or exercises.

Resources

These are not trainer or learning resources, but tools that will deepen your knowledge further in most of the areas covered by this book and add to your skills in business and at work (and often also in life).

Books

Backster, C. (2003) *Primary Perception: Biocommunication with plants, living foods and human cells.* Anza, CA: White Rose Millennium Press.
  The science behind talking to inanimate objects!

Buzan, Tony (2002) *How to Mind Map.* London: HarperCollins.
  An excellent introduction to mindmapping.

Charvet, S.R. (1997) *Words that Change Minds: Mastering the language of influence*, 2nd edition. Dubuque, IA: Kendall/Hunt Publishing Company.
  The definitive guide of the Language and Behaviour (LAB) Profile – a method of using language to influence and predict behaviour.

Dennison, G.E., Dennison, P.E. and Teplitz, J.V. (1994) *BrainGym for Business: Instant brain boosters for on-the-job success.* Ventura, CA: Edu-Kinesthetics, Inc.
  Contains the full set of moves, plus applications and suggested sequences.

Dilts, R. (1990) *Changing Belief Systems with NLP.* Capitola, CA: Meta Publications.
  A fairly technical, but useful, manual for structured belief change.

Gardner, H. (1999) *Intelligence Reframed: Multiple intelligences for the 21st Century.* New York: Basic Books.
  Fairly academic book giving the theory behind the multiple intelligences, including discussion of additional ones, including existential or spiritual.

Highmore Sims, N. (2005) *The Magical Business Name Machine.* Great

Yarmouth: www.bookshaker.com (e-book).
An interactive process for generating meaningful and creative names for businesses, services or products.

Knight, S. (1996) *NLP at Work*. London: Nicholas Brealey Publishing.
A very good practical introduction to neurolinguistic programming for those wishing to explore its potential before considering formal training.

Lakoff, G., and Johnson, M. (1980) *Metaphors We Live By.* Chicago: University of Chicago Press.
Though written by academics, an accessible book offering deeper insights into metaphor in daily life.

Meier, D. (2000) *The Accelerated Learning Handbook.* New York: McGraw-Hill.
What I consider to be the definitive work on accelerated learning for trainers and educators.

Tools

'Irresistible Influence' cards, Salad Ltd. www.saladltd.co.uk for online ordering.
Great tool for teaching yourself and others a different form of influencing language from that used in the LAB Profile.

MindManager software. www.mindmanager.com
Fairly intuitive software that allows you to generate mindmaps. The website has a free download so you can try it out before buying.

Learning music CDs/tools. www.anglo-american.co.uk
Lots of accelerated learning resources, including music and posters.

Websites and training

www.metaphizz.com

Nikki Highmore Sims (author): Master Practitioner in NLP and licensed LAB Profile consultant/trainer, offering training in workshop design and language patterns; excellence 'cloning' for sales and recruitment; and In-Vocation career change programme.

www.nlpu.com
US-based Internet home of Robert Dilts, one of the early developers of NLP and a phenomenal source of learning, resources and information.

www.peterhoney.com
Honey and Mumford's Learning Styles. Source of the profiling tool and further information on the styles for those interested in the deeper theory.

www.ppdlearning.co.uk
Excellent NLP Practitioner and Master Practitioner training, based in London and comprising a modular approach taught by many of the 'NLP greats' from the US and UK.

www.saladltd.co.uk
Jamie Stuart is a licensed NLP Trainer and Managing Director of Salad, an NLP training company and the world's leading resource of NLP products for linguistic skills – including the highly useful 'Salad cards'.

www.successtrategies.com (two not three Ss!)
Training in the LAB Profile available on both sides of the Atlantic by Shelle Rose Charvet.

Index